THE DOLPHIN WITHIN

THE DOLPHIN WITHIN

AWAKENING HUMAN POTENTIAL

OLIVIA DE BERGERAC PhD

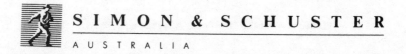

SIMON & SCHUSTER

AUSTRALIA

DEDICATIONS

To the baby seed who went with the whales
to allow me to follow my dream.
To my soul partner for bringing our
shared vision into reality.
To the dolphins, my teachers.

COVER PICTURE

A dolphin in the distinctive 'S' pose adopted
during courtship. (William McDougall)

THE DOLPHIN WITHIN

First published in 1998 by Simon & Schuster Australia
20 Barcoo Street, East Roseville NSW 2069

A Paramount Communications Company
Sydney   New York   London   Toronto   Tokyo   Singapore

ISBN 0 7318 0688 3

National Library of Australia
Cataloguing-in-Publication data

De Bergerac, Olivia.

The Dolphin Within

Includes index.
ISBN 0 7318 0688 3.

1. Dolphins – Psychic aspects. 2. Human-animal relationships.
3. Mental healing. I. Title

133.93

Printed by Australian Print Group, Maryborough, Victoria

The Dolphin Within is a registered propietary name of OBD Consulting Pty Ltd.

CONTENTS

PREFACE

This book is an account of our experiences with the dolphins. It is told through human stories, photos and drawings, transcripts of videos and conversations with participants of our Dolphin Within expeditions and through our research into human brain states before and after dolphin encounters. It integrates all the different ways we have used to capture the experience we call the Dolphin Within: the shared but intensely individual experiences people have when they are in close contact with wild dolphins.

Years ago, very few people in the western world talked about near death experiences; it's only since collective experiences have been gathered that we are now able to conceptualise this phenomenon more widely. Following the same approach, we have collected a large number of Dolphin Within experiences over the last three years, from our regular research trips during which we have witnessed many encounters between people and dolphins. Different patterns have emerged out of the 240 case studies, which show the power of transformation and healing that such encounters can create.

However, we went further than just collecting experiences; we tested our brains and those of participants before and after their Dolphin Within experiences, using an electroencephalograph (EEG) machine connected to a notebook computer. Using this method, we have found scientific evidence of and possible explanations for the changes in mind, body and spirit we have observed in people who encounter dolphins. The brainwave pattern changes that occur after a Dolphin Within experience are quite remarkable, and are linked to the self-transformation processes that many of our participants have reported.

One can say that our scientific research demystifies the healing power of dolphins. However, the more we observe, the more we realise how much we don't know, and the more we realise how much we People of the Earth have yet to learn from the People of the Sea.

This book explains why, since 1993, we have dedicated our lives, our financial resources and our time to the exploration of the human dolphin connection through the creation of the Dolphin Society, our non-profit institution, and ODB Consulting, our management consultancy. Both are aimed at bringing Dolphin Within experiences to the general public and to the business world. As management consultants, we have created a new psychology of human potential based on a dolphin model. Not only do we talk about the Corporate Dolphin way of doing business, but we also bring business people to experience the Dolphin Within themselves, in order to bring change in their personal and professional lives.

A Dolphin Within experience is indescribable, by definition. Every person coming out of a powerful experience with dolphins says the same thing: 'There are no words'. We ourselves don't even want to talk for some time after a Dolphin Within experience. So, creating a book about something that cannot be expressed in words is quite a challenge.

Until we humans develop a communication system similar to that of the dolphins (who share information with each other holographically, transferring images from brain to brain using sound), the written word, pictures and sounds are the best tools we have to offer a taste of the Dolphin Within experience to a wider audience. Our Internet page is another, more interactive way for us to share our explorations globally, and we are currently working on other ways to provide the healing and uplifting experiences dolphins can give us, without the intervention of dolphins themselves, in order to preserve their habitat and lifestyle.

We hope you will soon be able to hear, while reading, the 'ooh, hah whoo ha and Oh my God' which are part of any Dolphin Within experience. In 1994 we were asked by ABC Radio to put together some sounds of our trips for an interview, and we realised how much a Dolphin Within experience was about opening the heart and laughing, having the 'ho ha' human sounds coming out at each dolphin's jump at the bow of the boat.

Much of this book was written on the sea, on our yacht, with the dolphins around us. We just had to pop our heads out of the cabin, away from the computer screen, to spot a fin, even when the yacht was moored in the marina. We found that floating among dolphins was our best source of inspiration. We hope that this book will inspire you too to follow your dream.

Enjoy your Dolphin Within adventure, and come and join us one day!

Olivia and William
Sydney, 1997

1

THE LEGEND OF THE GOLDEN DOLPHIN

By Peter Shenstone, the Legendarian

Throughout the myth/history of civilisation runs a recurring theme. From time to time, at certain crucial turning points in humankind's journey from beast to self-awareness, there has occurred a mysterious communion with the 'people of the sea', the dolphins.

The record of this inspiring communion between the two great intelligent mammalian races on Earth, this 'space' contact, is encoded in the myths and legends handed down to us.

Whenever this has happened, a resulting spark of inspiration has illuminated the next phase of the civilising process, only to fade gradually from conscious memory ... until the next time.

As we pass through the current crisis of civilisation, tossed about in the creative chaos of the cusp between two ages, the door of perception is opening once again.

Now the ancient mythical tales make startling sense and take on dramatic new meaning as science begins to reveal the depth of the dolphins' significance.

Popular imagination is again fired with Delphic inspiration.

This is the Legend of the Golden Dolphin, the once and future story of our evolutionary dance of consciousness with the alien intelligence that inhabits the Oceanic vastness of our Spaceship Earth.

The dolphin's brain is larger and more complex than ours. Dolphins have access to both sides of their being, the logical and the intuitive, unlike people who are predominantly controlled by the left (logical) side of their brain. Dolphins have struck a balance between their obvious strength and obvious loving nature.

Living in the incredibly supportive environment of the sea, with access to three-quarter of the surface of the planet, and with larger, more intricate brains, the question becomes 'what are they doing down there?'

The hypothesis is that cetaceans — dolphins and whales — are a race of intelligent mammals many millennia in advance of humankind.

The fact that they are living in peace, without destroying the planet or declaring war on each other, suggest they are living in a state of grace. The sea-dwelling mammals have a lot to teach the predominant land-dwelling mammal, man, about that grace.

Myths and legends swim with dolphins guiding humanity toward civilisation. There are two intelligent races that share this planet; one race, the whales and dolphins, has been contacting humanity for thousands of years.

The connections take place at certain turning points in history, and we are going through a turning point now; the contact is happening again.

In the legends of India, civilisation was created when Vishnu, in the form of a fish man — actually a dolphin — arose from the Ganges River to help humankind. The early culture in the Cradle of Civilisation — Mesopotamia — had a similar fish god, which they called Oannes. In Greek mythology, Apollo turned into a dolphin and stopped a ship of merchants, telling them they would create an example for the human race for thousands of years to come, giving rise to the golden age of Greece.

Early Christians used the sign of a fish to mark their passing. Examination of those Christians' graves shows that the fish was actually a dolphin.

One African tribe, the Dogon people of Mali, has a very sophisticated knowledge of the star Sirius, the brightest star in the sky. They say it is a binary star (a fact only discovered by scientists in 1834) and they draw details of the movement of the two stars that match modern astronomy. The Dogon tell of having this knowledge from huge water creatures that breathe air and have flukes and who came from a planet in the Sirius system.

According to the Dogon, these creatures, the Nommo, will have one-third sacrificed on the altar of Human greed and insensitivity for the purification and reorganisation of the universe. Then the Nommo will arise in Human form and descend upon the Earth.

The 'resurrected' human dolphins will be gathered through the revelation of The Golden Dolphin into the Force of Freedom, inspired by and under the guidance thereof. The Legend of the Golden Dolphin says that the Force of Freedom will form itself upon the Island of Australia (one of the stars on the Australian flag is Sirius), which the Nommo have chosen for their return.

2

BECOMING A DOLPHIN CONSULTANT

Once upon a time, a little girl was born in the town of Antibes, on the famous French Riviera. Her mother, convinced she would have a third boy, didn't have a name ready for her. Her grandmother, who was impressed by her boss, an elegant lady from London, finally gave her the English name of Olivia. Olivia grew up with her two big brothers, lots of cousins and friends, by and in the sea. Her childhood was full of laughter and love, and people used to call her the 'daughter of the sun' because she was so full of light and life.

My life can be seen as a fairy tale. Psychiatrist Dr Eric Berne, the father of transactional analysis, says that every life is a kind of fairy tale, a predetermined script that we unconsciously compose and choose to follow during early childhood. The key is to be aware of the life script, to check if it is the one we want and to be able to change it. I ended up doing a PhD on that topic.

THE FIRST CALL

My favourite fairy tale was the Little Mermaid. I always felt that I had came out of the sea, falling in love with humans. Apparently, I was three when I jumped off a pontoon with my inflatable ring, and disappeared through it down into the big blue. My mother jumped in behind me and grabbed my long blond hair to bring me back to the surface. I was fine, she was green!

In my case, my whole family came out of the sea. We not only grew up by, on and in it, but before birth, in our mother's womb, we were in the sea a lot as she spent her spare time at the beach. We were all swimming and snorkelling by the age of five. My two brothers, Henry and Michel, lived in and for the sea, and learnt to scuba dive at the age of twelve. The 'Little Frenchman' in the film *The Big Blue* is a good portrait of my brothers.

At fifteen, my oldest brother Henry went to Monaco to see Jacques Cousteau's boat, *Calypso*. He touched it and said, 'One day, I'll be on board her'. At nineteen, he was organising expeditions to swim with and film whales and dolphins in the Mediterranean; I went along with him. At 22, Cousteau recruited him for his reputation and experience with whales and dolphins. He then worked in the Bahamas, Greece and finally Rapa Nui (Easter Island), where he and my other brother Michel ended up living.

I was quite a tomboy, living with such brothers. However, I knew very early that I was different from the other children. As a baby I had been very sick, and I nearly died twice before our family doctor discovered what was wrong with me: I had a hole in my heart.

I felt different and very mature, one could say like an old soul. At fifteen I had major heart surgery which, along with the physical heart pain, left me with a spiritual experience. I was back at school seven days after my surgery, with a strong optimism and a joy of being alive even more than before.

STUDIES, TRAVELS AND WORK

The second guiding principle in my life, after the sea, was studying. I loved school and enjoyed studying and teaching. I got a BAC D (the HSC equivalent) with maths, physics and biology. I wanted to study psychology at university, but I was accepted into the elite school of Grand Ecole Hypokhane et Khagne, which prepares French teachers and university professors. I enjoyed the studies and the monastic life for the first year and got some good marks, but I dropped my performance in the second year as it was becoming clearer that I didn't want to be a civil servant all my life (to the great disappointment of my mother!). I finished my studies at the University of Nice, combining French literature and psychology. I got a Bachelor of Arts, a Masters degree with a thesis on literature and psychoanalysis and a PhD on transactional analysis, looking at fairy tales as a life script.

The third guiding principle or value in my life since fifteen was love. I found great learning through loving. It was the way for me to learn about cultural differences and adaptation. I fell in love for the first time with a French martial arts teacher with an Italian background. At 21 I went to live in Paris and the United States with a half-French and half-American engineer. I then moved to London and later Australia with my third lover, an English engineer with a Greek background who became my husband.

Through this period I found a way to combine travel, study, work and love by designing language and cultural training courses for business executives. In France, large organisations like IBM, Dow Chemical and Schlumberger employed me to teach their expatriates employees about the French way of doing business, and how to adapt to the Parisian environment. In London I taught the executives of a French reinsurance company to speak French and to understand the French culture so that they could conduct negotiations with their parent company in Paris.

It was quite unusual in the 1970s for a young woman in her early twenties to be training senior executives in international organisations. I quickly realised that the key in my work was to find ways to help my clients to overcome their fear of learning, of failure. Behind this was a fear of being incompetent, a fear of not being a man (at that time there were not many women executives). My work was about creating a safe and enjoyable learning environment, where I could nurture their self-esteem.

I was helping my CEOs and top engineers to overcome their fears and to develop confidence in themselves. I was developing a strong relationship with them based on trust and mutual respect, playing the role of confidante. I knew about their work, their politics and their corporate culture, about their spouses, children and hobbies. In short, I was their psychotherapist, and I could see how business people needed one! Through my training, executives had better relationships at work and at home and better business results.

AUSTRALIA BECKONS

In 1988, a powerful awakening happened for me during a trip to Rapa Nui in the South Pacific, where my two brothers were living.

After having lived a yuppie life in Paris, the United States and London, it took me days and weeks to re-adapt to an adventurous life. I got kicked and left on the ground by a horse, attacked by the wild birds, lost in the volcano, and ran out of air in a 30 metre scuba dive. Meanwhile, I could see Michel, fit and tanned, disappearing into the sea on one breath of air for three minutes, followed by multicoloured fish. I could see Henry on top of an island getting closer and closer to a big, black wild bird to the point of touching without frightening it. My brothers, I realised, were alive, and living totally in harmony with nature.

As I was meditating by the famous Moais, the statues of Rapa Nui, I had a clear vision that my future would be in Australia. I knew that I needed to leave Europe, where I was planning to study for an MBA (Master of Business Administration). I saw that I needed to reconnect with my real values, a life by the sea in the South Pacific, and more studies in psychology.

MY MISSION INTO THE CORPORATE WORLD

Australia was home from the first day I arrived (25 September 1988). My new country embodies my principles of a multicultural society, natural resources and spiritual adventures. I began saying, I'm French by birth, but Australian by choice.

Soon after my arrival, I was teaching in the French Department of Sydney University, and I was doing some research in the Department of Economic History. I could have stayed there and followed an academic career, but I knew that my mission was in the corporate world.

Seven years in training with senior executives, counselling them on work and personal issues, had shown me that business leaders were driven by fear. I wanted to find ways to get rid of this fear. I knew that through the language and cultural training courses I had a huge impact on my clients' professional and personal lives. However, my skills were not recognised as those of an agent of change. I was also aware that my interventions were limited.

Wanting to understand management and business more deeply, and to gain more credibility in the corporate world, I began my MBA at the Australian Graduate School of Management (AGSM), with the intention of becoming a management consultant. It was quite an adventure. Everything was new for me. Completing the two-year full-time course in my second language, was a tremendous challenge. To add even more challenge, I began the first term with a divorce from my husband, who I had financially supported for two years in London while he was doing his MBA.

I left a comfortable life with a husband who was working for a prestigious consulting group. In order to pay for my studies, I sold my big diamond ring and continued working at Sydney University and later at AGSM in the export marketing department.

During this first term, I received first prize for a presentation. I used an exercise to enable my fellow students and our lecturer to experience a high level of communication in a non-competitive environment. During the activity I asked them to sit facing each other in pairs, making eye contact while listening to music in a candle-lit environment, in order to connect heart to heart beyond the competitive MBA culture.

Throughout my studies, I challenged the establishment and the AGSM system. I wrote a paper entitled 'The Harvardian Strait Jacket' in which I exposed the limitations of the American business school model. Having taught MBA students from London Business School and INSEAD (the Paris business school), I had been exposed to the European business school model, which was more open to a wide range of international management practices. My understanding of cultural diversity enabled me to argue the limitation of transferring American management practice to the international arena. I denounced the American MBA dictatorship that ignores the different ways of doing business in various parts of the world, and assumes that if you can sell cars in New York, you will be successful at selling cars in India. I wrote that Australian multiculturalism could be an asset rather than a liability, if we could capitalise on it and use it for export. Australian business schools could create a powerful model for the rest of the world.

I did an individual study called 'e=mc² (Exporting Equals Multicultural Competences Squared)', which attracted the marketing professor's attention. He asked me to become his research assistant in the AGSM Centre of Export Marketing. I also presented papers at international conferences in Japan and Malaysia, the first one on a management simulation and the second on cross-cultural management. I was travelling in Asia while other students were painfully competing to get the best marks.

I think I represented a new breed of MBA student; I became a role model for some students. I didn't want to be destroyed by the MBA culture of hard work, competition and no private life. I didn't drink alcohol or smoke, I didn't take tea or coffee or any drugs. My drug was early morning swimming, yoga and meditation.

The morning of my finance exams, I went swimming in the surf. It was winter and very few people were at the beach. I got caught in the strong surf, and nearly drowned. On the way to the school, I was so happy to be alive that my fear of the exam evaporated completely. I got a distinction.

I had passionate discussions at the school. One day I had a long debate with a student friend, David. He was from an Anglo-Saxon background but he had lived in Papua New Guinea since he was a baby, and he was a scuba diver like me. David was doing a cost benefit analysis of drilling the Great Barrier Reef. I asked him about the results of his calculation.

'Did you find out that it was not a proper investment?' I asked.

'No, it was okay to drill the reef', he said.

'How could you possibly get such a result? What dollar value did you put on the reef?'

'Well, none. The reef has no value.'

I was amazed. 'How can you say that, you who are a diver? Did you use your knowledge of the reef, your love for diving when you were writing your assignment? Did you listen to your heart while you were calculating?'

He thought for a moment. 'No, it isn't possible to use the mind and the heart simultaneously. I had to put aside my passion for the reef.'

I replied, 'It's people like you, combining an economics background with an understanding of the environment, who can create new measurements, different from a cost benefit analysis, by putting a value on the environment. It's by combining our different backgrounds that we can be unique and add to the field of research, to the community and to the world. By cutting off your heart, you've limited yourself to the traditional way of calculating, and you've missed an opportunity to bring new light into the approach!'

Another topic I was passionate about was teaching cultural differences to business people in order to broaden their views as global managers. I knew how important it was to understand and value cultural differences in order to run businesses internationally. I could see that training business people without an understanding of the other cultures was not developing global managers of the 21st century. Even Australian managers have, without any doubt, increasingly multicultural workforces.

A student friend from Hong Kong told me one day: 'Olivia, you are always saying that it's great to have different cultural backgrounds. It's easy for you, because you're French. Me and my friends from Hong Kong, we get stones thrown at us in the street'.

I had no answer to that point. I knew that there was a lot of work to be done, and that I wanted to create workshops where cultural differences, and any other differences in gender, age, size, colour of skin and so on could be transcended. Places where the universality and individuality of being human could shine. One day it will happen.

SECOND CALL

The Australian dolphins made contact with me in Sydney in winter 1990. Living in Coogee, I went for my early morning swim, as I do every day of the year. On this particular occasion, it was a Sunday and as I arrived at the beach I spotted some dolphins in the bay. I immediately jumped into the water to join them, feeling they were waiting for a human contact. I was the only swimmer.

I swam towards them, but they disappeared. I stayed in the water, and about ten or fifteen minutes later I was surrounded by six dolphins that swam around me. I stayed with them for an hour in the water with no wetsuit. I was completely frozen, but so happy and joyful! What struck me in that encounter (beyond a very strong smell of fish and a sense of feeling alive) was the certitude of having reconnected with something very important for me.

I came out of the water and I was in shock for some months. After fifteen years of studies, my experience with the dolphins had awakened something deep, very deep in me; something that I had never read about in any book of psychology or even esotericism.

However, it was rather difficult to share my experience with my peers, who were training to be bankers, stockbrokers or management consultants.

Between Accounting and New Venture Planning lectures, it was rather difficult to say: 'Hi guys, by the way, I swam with dolphins last weekend and it's just extraordinary. It gives you an inner peace that transcends all human experience'.

I was weird enough already, being the only French student, riding a motorbike, with a PhD, not drinking alcohol, coffee or tea, not smoking, but meditating and managing to study full time and work part time.

Apart from my business career, I was a student at Clairvision, a transpersonal psychotherapy school in Sydney. No one there could understand the dolphin effect I was talking about either! I felt even more different.

The only person who knew what I was talking about was Peter Shenstone, who I met through a friend. Peter was living in the Blue Mountains, away from the corporate world. We spent an afternoon together and he told me about the *Legend of the Golden Dolphin*. Peter was working in advertising and marketing when he started to question the fact that he was helping his clients to sell products (like cigarettes) which were destroying the health of the consumers and the health of the planet. In 1983, after a profound connection with dolphins through a meditation, Peter left his successful marketing career to research and share around the world the legend: a collection of factual, mythical, historical and religious stories of human dolphin encounters. I listened to him with great attention and respect. I kept my own experience in my heart for the next three years.

BECOMING A TQM CONSULTANT

It was during an AGSM career night that I met John, my future boss. During his presentation, he communicated his personal vision. He talked about his business but also the human side of the business, his family, his learning through cancer, his personal challenge in life. I knew that I had found a place to start my work.

After finishing the MBA, I joined John's company. John said he was told from the business school, that 'Olivia changed the AGSM more than the school changed her'.

For the next two years working as a Total Quality Management consultant, I increased my knowledge of organisational change. I introduced to my new company innovative ways of collecting information (one using the Roadrunner cartoon!) on the values of an organisation. I designed and developed team training and leadership training programs using outdoor activities in order to develop trust, self-confidence and teamwork in business organisations.

TAKING RISKS IN CONSULTING

Working with John on a large project for an Australian building construction group, I was in charge of the employee survey and running focus group sessions. I had to fly all over Australia in order to collect information, visiting road, tunnel and building sites. I then organised a three-day vision setting and strategic planning workshop for the 27 executives.

I had prepared a workbook with the statistics, the comments and the drawings collected from the focus group sessions. I divided the group into teams, each looking at different state and overseas results. The task was to analyse the results and make a presentation after dinner.

After dinner the group was relaxing, throwing golf balls into the sea, as we were in a conference centre facing the ocean. I let them play for a while and then asked them to come back to the room. As they returned the MD told me, 'Olivia, you only have ten minutes to finish. The bar opens in ten minutes'.

I had a flashback of a drawing I had not included in the feedback presentation. A young lady had drawn a huge bottle of wine as a metaphor for the organisation. She explained to me that the organisational culture was just about drinking (typical in that industry).

I had three seconds to intervene, otherwise the voices of the employees would be forgotten. I had made a commitment to them. I could also understand that the executives had difficulties looking at the results, which were not very positive.

I faced the 27 men and said, 'We have reached an important stage of the workshop. We have two options. One is to forget about it and go drinking. Some people do that when they reach an obstacle. The other is to go on and complete the task. It's up to you to choose.'

I just wanted to mirror their behaviour, to show them that they had choices in life. Retrospectively I wish I had given them a third option, which would have been to finish the task and then to enjoy the drinks. I don't like the either/or that presents a dilemma, while three options give real choices.

There was a big silence in the room. I could see my boss John looking at me. His face was as white as the wall, he looked close to fainting. This was our biggest contract for any client. Just for my part, I had billed $40 000 in a month. The cheque we got that month had six figures. John had photocopied it and framed it in his office. He was so happy. I was challenging the client now, and jeopardising the contract.

I wanted to give voice to the truth. I was ready to defend the people's voice and risk my own position. In a fraction of a second, I could see John's thinking, I evaluated the risk I was taking and I saw the MD's eyes. I was waiting for a miracle!

I got a long silence, in French one says: 'an angel passes' or 'we could hear the flies flying' (in English, 'we could hear a pin drop').

And suddenly, the Human Resources Manager stood up and shouted, 'We'll follow you!'

They all become excited about finishing the task and facing the things the employees were saying about the company. We finished at 11 p.m. and then went for drinks.

At the end of the workshop, the MD said to me, 'Thank you, Olivia. Now I understand why you insisted on the employee surveys.'

The following month, he made the same tour I had made around Australia to give feedback to the employees, using the key figures and the key drawings. Following the employees' recommendations, he made the necessary changes: new directions, restructuring, training.

THE MAGIC OF THE LITTLE BAY

Late that night, as everyone was drinking, I went to the beach. Peter, the number two in our company, soon followed me. I was sitting by the water in a little bay where I used to scuba dive at night. The night was magic, there was a full moon and the sky was full of stars. Peter said, 'You took a big risk with the group. How did you know it would work?'

'I trust', I said.

'You trust yourself?'

'I trust the people in the group', I replied.

We walked together on the beach. Peter shared his life story, he told me he was thinking of leaving his job, his wife. I was listening. Then my boss John joined us. He also felt the magic of the bay, and started to talk from his heart about his childhood.

When he left, Peter said to me, 'You know, I have never got close to John, but tonight he talked so simply. I've discovered another John'.

I knew then that my mission was to create space where business people could be themselves without the facade and the sea was part of the process.

LEARNING WITH FUN

I initiated Peter to the world of computers. After that night, Peter and I began to jog along the beach as a way to conduct business meetings. One day, after a jog and a drink in a little cafe, I brought out my notebook computer and let him play with the Treasury function. Again I was using my approach about learning through playing, the best way to overcome any fear. After a few weeks, Peter said: 'You know, Olivia, I am using my own computer now to write my letters, I want to go on a course to learn more.'

My eyes were full of joy, and he added, 'I knew it would make you happy'.

Peter often talked about the friendship we had. I had to remind him that it was work. He admitted that he was learning. 'I've learnt a lot from you, you always give me ideas and articles, books to read. I like talking to you. I feel good just talking to you.'

By that time, I was aware that I was fostering my client's learning not just with my brain for strategic thinking, my creativity for innovative ideas, my French accent for relaxing their minds, I was giving them my energy, my life force. I was like a battery of energy; by staying with me they felt recharged and happy.

I was certainly different from the mainstream consultant, but this was nothing compared with what was going to happen to me the following year when I heard the third call and reconnected with the dolphins. Challenging the establishment was one thing, but becoming a corporate dolphin consultant was something else.

THE THIRD CALL

The third call from the dolphins was going to transform my life. I had received the university training. I had all the qualifications and credibility. I had read a lot of books, I had been trained in many disciplines, from mainstream TQM consulting to less orthodox psychotherapy. The techniques I was using in psychotherapy were indeed far from the university books. They are very powerful tools to explore different states of consciousness, but I was going to experience something stronger, an even more effective way of getting in touch with my higher self.

The entire purpose of my work as a management consultant and a psychotherapist was to find ways to help individuals, teams and organisations to change, not just for the sake of changing, but to be more themselves. To be free from cultural, family and society conditioning, to tap into their full potential, to find their purpose, make real choices in life and bring their visions into reality.

What I was going to experience with the dolphins would be so strong that, finally, I wouldn't be able to deny it or forget about it any longer. I would put aside all the books, university studies and training I had received over the past fifteen years to start from scratch, as a student in year one at the dolphin school!

3

DISCOVERING MY PURPOSE IN LIFE

On my thirty-third birthday, the 2 December, I left Sydney at five in the morning to go to Port Stephens with one goal: to swim with wild dolphins. I knew I could see them in Port Stephens. I had run two management workshops there, and I had seen a boat with a sign saying 'Dolphin Watch'. Each time, though, I had been unable to leave my clients to go and meet the dolphins. My birthday gift to myself was to see them and swim with them.

As a management consultant with a good salary, I could have gone to Bali, to Club Med, or bought myself any expensive gift. However I knew that my only real joy would be to swim again with wild dolphins.

When I arrived and saw the few different boats and the ferry that ran dolphin watch trips for tourists, I knew that I would not be able to experience the dolphins with a large group of noisy tourists. I also knew that no captain would allow me to swim from his boat, due to safety regulations and insurance considerations. My emergency plan was to fall into the water 'by accident'.

My first plan was to hire a skippered boat, to be free to do whatever I wanted. I was told by the guy in the booking office, 'You can't hire a boat and a skipper here!' He looked at me as though I was crazy.

From the beginning of my story with dolphins in Australia, I have been told again and again, 'it's not possible'. Thousands of times I have heard the same answer or comment, 'you can't do that'. I have learnt to overcome other people's fears in order to follow my dream. How many people have been told that about their dream?

I left the booking office, unshaken by the look of the guy and on the way out, I saw *Orca*, a motor sailer with a sign on the mast that said 'Hire Me'. *Orca* is the name of my brothers' adventure and filming company on Rapa Nui. I knew then it was *Orca* I needed. I called the captain. He came straight away and we left the marina. Ian was his name. He was happy to let me do whatever I wanted.

Orca is a ten-metre motor sailer with a broad beam, very stable. I was on the bow deck, watching for dolphins, when I reconnected with a very important part in me: the adventurer. This part will not die, despite my job as a management consultant. As soon as I am on a boat a little voice says, 'You belong to this world'.

This same voice came to me while I was on Rapa Nui two years before on my brothers' boat. We were going scuba diving and my inner voice said, 'You belong in this world, you can't stay in an office. Don't get trapped; your mission is to bring adventure to the business world.'

Facing the sea, I was looking for dolphin fins when another flashback came to my mind: another trip with my brother. I was around fifteen, and I was with my elder brother Henry, before he joined the Cousteau Society, filming dolphins and whales in the Mediterranean. My role was to look from a platform on the top of the mast for signs of dolphins or whales, and to take photos of them. I remembered the feeling when my heart stopped for a second as I saw dolphin fins. I could hear myself shouting, 'dolphins, dolphins' to my brothers who were at the bow.

On *Orca*'s deck, I was reflecting on how important it is to spend time looking for dolphins. It's like a quest. They come when we are ready, only when we really appreciate their presence. I started to call the dolphins from my heart, and then, suddenly, I spotted a fin. I could feel them before seeing them. The same joy, the same shout as when I was fifteen, 'Dolphins!'

I jumped. I always jump in the air when I see dolphins. It's such a gift, such a joy!

SHARING THE EXPERIENCE

They came straight to the boat. I put a snorkelling mask and swim fins on, and got into the water. They were in deep sea, and I started swimming. The strongest memory I keep from this first swim in Port Stephen was the sounds of the dolphins underwater. Such bliss! It was a reconnection with something deep inside me. I spent an hour in the water with them around me. They stayed about seven metres away from me. It was obvious that they weren't used to seeing swimmers. I didn't want to chase them, I just wanted to swim in their waters and listen to them.

This time, nothing could stop me from following my connection with dolphins. I was ready to take any risks necessary, to face any changes in my life. I had no study or work constraints, no reputation to preserve, no husband or family life to conform to, no financial fears. Nothing could stop me. I was ready to commit myself totally to understanding more about the phenomenon I was experiencing and share it with others.

Back on *Orca*, I was clear about what I had to do. I had to come back, I had to share the experience with friends and others. It would be soon, within two weeks. I could feel it. I had to organise a group to go and see dolphins, and I would initiate them to snorkelling and scuba diving.

Back home, I designed in one night a program I called 'The Dolphin Within'.

THE DOLPHIN WITHIN PROGRAM

Enjoy a weekend with dolphins at Port Stephen, 18-19 December 1993.

Workshop Activities

Swimming in the dolphins' environment, sailing, snorkelling, scuba diving (introductory course), one night on board, breakfast, lunches, dinner, equipment for snorkelling, equipment for diving, transport from Sydney.

Bring:
swimmers, towel, sun block cream, zinc, hat, sunglasses, jumpers, raincoat, your passion or dream to share with the group.
Pack everything in a soft bag (except the dream!)

I gave this little flier to my friends at the school of psychotherapy, and within a week I had my group. I only had to following the impulse, and everything was organised.

THE FIRST DOLPHIN WITHIN PROGRAM

The first Dolphin Within program was more than encouraging. The group was quite diverse, with two young girls of eighteen (Olivia and Georgina), a woman of fifty (Glen), a young guy of twenty-three (Matteus), and a man of thirty-eight (William). We were four from the school of psychotherapy, and four from outside the school, including Michael the diving instructor and Ian the captain of the boat.

Arriving at the marina, I organised a swim, the group had its first contact with water, and we ate mangoes for breakfast!

SONGS TO THE DOLPHINS

We then left the marina and started looking for dolphins. There was a shared desire in the group, a deep desire to meet the dolphins, and together we started singing to attract them. Matteus and William had beautiful voices. Our call was rising from the flow. It was full of respect for the dolphins' mission. Soon, the dolphins came. It was a beautiful connection and a revelation for all of us. A very strong heart energy flowed between us. It was a unique moment in life, which bonded the group. It was like observing a miracle together; there was suddenly a long silence, and we held our breath.

Then I went swimming in their world. I enjoyed swimming in the deep sea; when I came back to the boat I realised that the dolphins were teaching me how to let go of desire. They came when I stopped wanting them, when I gave them the space to come to me.

After admiring the dolphins, our little group had a beautiful energy. It was time to snorkel and experience the Dolphin Within. The group (made up of people who loved the sea, but were scared to put their heads under water) had forgotten their fear, and discovered the pleasure of seeing the underwater world. Slowly they started swimming and going underwater as I was doing my dolphin swim dance.

Since my first swim with the Port Stephens dolphins, a swim, a dolphin dance, has inhabited my body. It's a little bit like the butterfly stroke but I do it partly underwater, imitating the dolphins' movements. It just came with a sound, and I feel great when I do it. It cleanses me entirely. I feel pure and joyful. I have observed that when people see me dancing they start doing it as well, connecting with their Dolphin Within.

Once the group felt comfortable with the new snorkelling equipment, we went to feed the fish. The group really enjoyed the contact with water and the marine life. Feeding fish is a fantastic gesture. We were in a marine reserve, where no one can fish. As soon as humans stop killing them, the animals are friendly. They ate from our hands, a beautiful experience.

When we went scuba diving, I realised that my mission was really to connect people with their Dolphin Within, watching them overcome fears. Diving was a sublime pleasure. I decided to become a diving instructor because I wanted to share that first initiation with people underwater. I have observed that something quite important happens under water. It's like a reconnection with the inner-self. I wanted to be there and facilitate the reconnection between humans and the sea: a new initiation.

A POSEIDON STORY

Later, I asked William what happened for him over the weekend.

I heard you speaking of your experience on the day of your birthday. On the way back you stopped over at the Psychotherapy School, and you talked about the dolphins. I knew then I would come on the trip. I don't feel okay in the water. I nearly drowned once when I was a kid, so I've never felt comfortable swimming. It was a frightening experience at the time, and when I'm in the water the memory comes back and I can't breathe properly.

During the weekend, my first impression was related to the boat. It was such a beautiful boat. I reconnected with some past memories I have put aside; memories of sailing, and my father's love for boats.

Then there was the process of the group connecting with each other while we were getting away from the marina. As soon as we got outside the marina, we started to feel like a group cast off from the rest of the world. There was a sense of adventure. I didn't know what the weekend was about but I was excited.

Singing for the dolphins was special. They were protecting us. Seeing the dolphins was so beautiful. Even just seeing them from a distance. I didn't expect to feel that feeling of love, of opening in my heart. I was expecting to feel excited. I had read a little bit about dolphins' encounters with humans, but this was something unexpected. Seeing you jumping in the water, swimming with them, so much like a dolphin yourself, so much at home, so natural; my heart went out to you too.

After that experience, I was amazed. It brought something into the group. I felt much more open. The dolphins did that to the group. I know they did that.

Then we sailed and snorkelled. It was beautiful to feed the fish, the experience of being underwater was very special. It was the first time I'd got close to such animals in their own environment. Being under the waves with the fish is another world. It was a taste of what was to come the next day.

As we sailed, the whole energy of the boat changed. I was suddenly no longer fighting. It changed our energy, too. It put something into us. Watching the sunset from the little boat was special, too.

Then we had a fire on the beach; I sang some songs. I enjoyed it, it was my turn to give something to the group. Something I haven't done for a long time. I forgot how good it can be, everybody loves to join in and sing a song.

Sleeping on the beach under the stars was beautiful. The peaceful feeling of the bay. The water was so still. In the morning, the air was so clear after the night.

Then we sailed again. We saw more dolphins. We didn't go too close but even so I got the feeling of being invited into their world.

We moved into diving. Diving was such an amazing experience. To be able to stay under water, to be able to see. It was like being transported into another world. Seeing it first hand, seeing it myself, very different from seeing it on film. Seeing and feeling part of it is amazing. I didn't want to come up to the surface again. I just wanted to stay there. I was so happy. It was a new experience, I wanted to explore more. There was so much in it.

We then had a fantastic sail back to the marina. It was very windy. There was a feeling of being one with the sea. Not fighting. We were stronger. The biggest gift was to see a dolphin on the way back to the marina, so beautiful, so close, coming to say goodbye.

None of us wanted to leave. Overall we had a beautiful time. A time to learn new things about the sea. The sea has given us some of its secrets; things I have never felt before.

BREAKING THROUGH LIMITS

An evaluation of the program gave some interesting results. It was possible to take individuals like William, who couldn't feel comfortable in water due to a childhood trauma, or Glen, who couldn't swim, and create an adventure with the dolphins to facilitate a breakthrough of their fears or self-limitations. However, the process was about more than just overcoming fear; there was something about following a dream and experiencing a state of peace.

At that time, I didn't know how it worked, but I knew that others shared a unique experience. I was not the only one sensitive to the dolphin effect. I knew that the dolphins played an important role and that the program was producing surprising results, but I had no idea how to explain the phenomenon. I wanted to bring more people with different fears or health problems and just experiment, looking for ways to measure and understand the Dolphin Within experience.

That first result was enough to confirm to me that I had found my purpose in life. My family background, my studies in psychology and business, my spiritual work and my move to Australia were part of a big plan to bring me to research dolphin/human encounters. With my background I would be able to design a research program to investigate these experiences on the physiological, psychological and spiritual levels. I would find a way to use the latest technology to help measure the effect.

What had been until now different pieces of a puzzle became a huge mosaic that started to make sense. I saw how I could make a difference on the planet. I saw my uniqueness. I saw why I had been through so many traumas and adventures that often at the time did not make sense. I suddenly had a plan, a purpose. I realised that once you have your purpose it's easy to make decisions and choices. Life becomes a flow.

I realised I could help others find their reason for being. I could support individuals, teams and whole organisations to find their purpose and uniqueness.

THE RESEARCH PROGRAM

I had a clear plan of the research I wanted to conduct even if I didn't know how to do it, scientifically and financially. The plan I put on paper was as follows:

> The Dolphin Within research program is a long-term project that aims to study the impacts on human beings of contact with dolphins. The central theme of the project is to identify the physiological, psychological and spiritual changes people go through when they watch dolphins and/or swim with them.

The program is based on world research and our own personal experiences with dolphins. It investigates three basic hypotheses:

1. It is possible to create a learning space with dolphins as a 'medium' to aid the learning process.
2. People, including those with physical or mental problems, can receive benefits from contact with dolphins.
3. Dolphins have a healing power that acts on people on various levels (physical, psychological and spiritual).

The research program has three components: a pre-workshop session, the workshop itself and follow-up sessions.

In the pre-workshop session, participants are interviewed to establish their relationship with the ocean and water, and to examine their physiological and psychological profiles. They undergo tests designed to assess their physical health and fitness and pre-experiment brainwave patterns.

A two-day workshop is conducted on a sailing boat in safe waters near Sydney. The workshop includes activities such as sailing, dolphin watching, and snorkelling, swimming with dolphins and an introductory scuba dive. Participants stay overnight on the boat. We assess participants' brainwave patterns and other physiological indicators before, during and after contact with dolphins.

Following the workshop, participants are contacted regularly over a minimum of a year for interviews, questionnaires, journal analysis and group sessions.

The research is mainly qualitative, and uses the following tools: in-depth interview sessions, physiological and psychometric tests, brainwave reading, drawings, journals, photos and video recording.

The results will be published in three formats; articles for medical or research journals and general news/magazine media, a series of video films, a book, documentary films and a fiction film. Electronic means of communication such as the Internet will also be used extensively.

The different categories of people involved in the workshop include: people who have phobias about the sea, sharks, snorkelling, scuba diving etc.; people with depression; people with physical or mental disabilities of various forms; and people in quest of self-development and self-transformation, including business people.

THE RESEARCH LICENCE

I went to see the NSW National Parks and Wildlife Service in order to get a research licence to be able to have people swimming with dolphins. Everyone told me that the person in charge was a very dry, closed and strict person. I sent him my research plan by mail and then went to see him to explain the purpose of the research.

He didn't let me finish my first sentence, saying: 'You don't have to tell me, my grand-daughter had a chance to swim with dolphins recently [in a pool] and she hasn't stopped talking about it since. I know exactly what you are talking about. My only concern is that if your research is too successful, it might put too much pressure on the dolphins.'

I said, 'I share your concern, that's why the research aims at finding the key elements that provide the healing, so that we can reproduce it without the presence of the dolphins.'

We made an agreement and I reaffirmed that we would always respect and protect the dolphins. They were to come first in the equation of dolphin human encounters.

Behind the closed and reserved 'authority' person, I had connected with a charming man and we had really shared the dolphin message together. When I left his office, I thanked in my mind his grand-daughter, who had made the dolphin connection for me.

4

I WAS THE FIRST GUINEA PIG

CHRISTMAS DAY WITH THE DOLPHINS

On Christmas Eve in 1993, I left Sydney after work to travel to Port Stephens. I had a meeting with myself. It was to be the first Christmas I had spent alone in my life. Different friends had invited me to spend Christmas with them, but I wanted to be alone with the sea and the dolphins. William, my friend from the first Dolphin Within trip, had lent me his four-wheel-drive so I could go and see the dolphins, as he was flying to Melbourne to visit his three children who lived with his ex-wife.

I slept on *Orca's* deck in the marina that night, and spent Christmas Day at the beach. I couldn't find any boats to go out on, as it was Christmas and the skippers were with their families. I let go of my desire to swim with the dolphins, with a voice inside telling me, 'This time they might come and see you.'

I walked, swam, read and really enjoyed the beauty of the beach, the sea and this new feeling inside me — calmness, knowingness, peace.

Around five o'clock in the evening, I packed my gear and left the Shoal Beach to spend some time at a Little Beach. I had a deep feeling that dolphins would be there. As soon as I got close to the water, I saw their fins. The dolphins were very close to the beach. I put on my mask and swim fins and swam with the dolphins from 6 p.m. till 9 p.m. In the dark, I could see and feel their fins coming straight to me. I wasn't able to touch them but they came very close to me, perhaps less than one metre away.

That was the most beautiful Christmas Day of my life. The deep insight which came to me was, 'Dolphins, like Christ a long time ago, are bringing a new love consciousness onto the planet, they are coming to humans to announce a new way of being, a new way for us to relate to each other. However, it isn't a new religion. It isn't about believing and dividing people but experiencing *within*. Everyone can relate to a dolphin, whatever their skin colour, language, culture, religion, gender, age etc. They are facilitating the new planetary and global consciousness which is coming'.

A QUICK ESCAPE TO THE DOLPHINS

On Boxing Day, I drove back to Sydney. I met William at the airport and we both drove west into the mountains for a meditation retreat. We were to spend three days there, followed by a day's break, then another seven days of intensive meditation back in Sydney.

On the way to the bush, I said to William, 'I want to go back to the dolphins in the day we have between the two workshops'.

Three days later, as we were leaving the bush, William asked me, 'Do you still want to go to the dolphins?'

'Yes', I said.

'So, let's go!'

We drove straight to Port Stephens, and we saw dolphins in the same little beach that evening. We watched the full moon rising from the sea, we made a fire, and William played the guitar. We spent the night sleeping on the beach. Another blessed night.

In the morning we went across the bay on a passenger boat. I said to William, 'We have to find dolphins for the captain'.

I had hardly finished my sentence when I saw a fin not far away. I showed the captain and went to the front deck. I opened my heart and the dolphin came straight towards me and played under the bows, belly up. It was a beautiful gift. I wanted to jump. William held me. I wanted to go back and play more with them, but the captain had a schedule. I said to William, 'Soon we'll be back with *Orca,* so we can do whatever we want. One day we'll have our own boat and play as much as we want with the dolphins'.

Later, William shared his feelings at that time:

> There was an incredible impulse after the workshop in the bush. It felt very important to get back to the sea, to the dolphins. Something was pulling me. I knew it was something you wanted to do. I wanted to make it possible, to see the way it lights you up.
>
> You saw dolphins straight away. Seeing the effect in you, how the contact with dolphins opens something. How much at home you were. That was beautiful to see. Then, finding a beach and a spot for the night. The full moon was amazing, rising up from the water. It just felt right, because it was so spontaneous. Time just flowed beautifully. There was no grasping, just the enjoyment of doing it and creating our own event.

My intuition told me that we had to organise a weekend with William's children, Clare, Rory and James. I had never met them. I knew they were coming from Melbourne for a holiday with their father soon. I felt that it was important for them to be connected with the dolphins.

Two weeks later we were back!

MY NEW FAMILY

Children have an incredible connection with dolphins. Clare, Rory and James were full of joy when they saw them. On the first morning, sailing on *Orca*, twenty dolphins came towards us. What bliss!

Rory asked me, 'Why are you making that noise?'.

I was 'whistling' in the way I'd heard the dolphins do it. 'I'm talking to them!'

The children started to whistle with me.

I asked, 'What did you feel, Clare, with the dolphins?'.

'I felt happy', she replied.

The dolphin trip with William's children opened several doors. First of all I realised that I have to bring children to the dolphins. I was also certain that I wanted to share my life with William. The insight I got was that he was the person with whom I could share the dolphin work. I had reached a point in my life where I didn't want to have a relationship. I was determined to stay single for one year, to put my energy into my personal development and into my dolphin connection.

I had been in love and been loved a lot, and I had learnt a lot from my relationships. My first lover taught me everything about martial art (judo, karate and self-defence). My second lover taught me about computers and sailing. My husband had awakened my sexuality when I was 24 (it was time) and given me the idea to do an MBA. I was looking for something different from the usual romantic, physical, intellectual love. In fact I was not looking for anything human. I had reached the point of enjoying being by myself with the dolphins.

William was a friend for me, we were both students of the same psychotherapy school. He had joined the school three years after me and we were just friends. He had split up with his girlfriend about the same time that I had left my partner, promising myself a year on my own.

One night I received a call from William, he offered me the following deal: 'Olivia, if you want a relationship without any mess, we can have one together, and explore another way!'

At that time I laughed. I couldn't believe that he was asking me directly on the phone to go out with him. I was shocked by his lack of romanticism. I laughed and said that I didn't want a relationship.

During the following months, we saw each other as friends, we went camping together in the bush for our meditation training organised by School. I saw him as a big brother, and I felt safe because I wasn't physically attracted to him. We were doing things together, we were close friends, sharing experiences without having a sexual relationship.

I didn't want to fall in love. Instead I was discovering a deeper love based on a strong friendship, a knowingness of each other and a total acceptance of where we both were. I was not falling in love; I was rising in love. The dolphin work brought us together, and our love grew out of each dolphin experience we shared. On the boat with William and the children, I felt we were a family. The energy was very high and something connected in us. It was as though they were my pod.

Later William told me that Clare had asked him on the boat, 'When are you going to marry Olivia?'

'I don't think she is the marrying kind', he had said.

'You should!' she had replied.

I had only spent two days with these children, but something had happened. We knew that it was serious, even if we were all laughing. The connection was made at the level of our souls. The night of the dolphin weekend with the children, William and I naturally fell asleep in each other's arms. While little James was sleeping next to us, we just started to kiss each other, and we spent the whole night cuddling.

At that time I was still not physically attracted to William but I was energetically attracted to him. It's difficult to explain, but it was as if my energy body was linked with his. There was a harmony between us, something that I had never experienced before.

The dolphins were witnesses of our relationship, and they blessed it. However, as I had promised myself to stay alone for a year, I asked William to be patient for many more months before we could make love.

MONKEY MIA CALLS US

When I started to talk about my idea of running workshops for business people on yachts so they could learn about team building and other things, my boss looked at me askance. I knew that my position in the company was at risk. I was not fitting the mould. I knew that I had to follow my dream and that nothing could stop me.

The day I resigned from my management-consulting job, William told me that he had a project to run in Perth, and he asked me if I would like to go with him. I quickly thought, 'Perth — Monkey Mia — yes, I do!'

I realised how the timing of my resignation was perfect.

Since our dolphin connection, William had started to receive very convenient assignments in dolphin places such as Perth, Byron Bay, and so on. We went, and William spent a week working in Perth on a transport-planning project while I spent a week swimming with dolphins. I went to Rockingham, and I swam with the dolphins in Bunbury.

I was driving fast in the hire car one afternoon, trying to reach Bunbury before sunset. I was alone on a very long, straight road which was red, the colour of the sand. Suddenly I saw another car, coming very fast in the opposite direction. When it got closer, I realised it was an unmarked police car but it was already too late for me to slow down.

The guy passed me, made a U-turn, and chased me. I stopped, and as he was writing me a fine, he asked me, 'Do you have a valid reason for driving so fast?'

I said, 'Yes, I'm going to swim with dolphins!'

Not surprisingly he didn't find that a valid excuse, and I got a $120 fine.

On the Friday night we went to a cocktail party with some of William's clients. We explained to these transport consultants and public servants that we were going to drive overnight the 900 kilometres to Monkey Mia to swim with dolphins. Moreover, we were going to drive back on Sunday night to take a plane to Sydney, to be back at work on Monday morning. They looked at us as though we were crazy. Most of them had lived all their lives in Perth, but few had ever driven to Monkey Mia.

They were looking at me with curious eyes, a little bit uncomfortable with this French 'girl' (and all the cliches you can imagine about French girls) who was taking away their Anglo-Saxon, conscientious transport engineering consultant, who had worked 23 years with the same company. William was known for his world expertise, his calmness, and his respectable and quiet life. They knew he was divorced, but that can happen nowadays. But what was this story about a dolphin experience?

William did drive the whole night, and we arrived at a beach, we were not sure which one. We parked and slept on the sand, to be wakened by the sun rising and the dolphins coming. We had found Monkey Mia. I went swimming with the dolphins as soon as they left the tourist area where they get fed, and I had a very powerful experience that opened my mind to the potential healing power of dolphins.

HEALING MY HEART

I've never been particularly delicate and fragile. As a child, I was more or less a tomboy, playing with my brothers and their friends rather than with girls' toys. I knew I had been very sick as a baby, and nearly died twice. I also knew that I was different because I had a hole in my heart. The family doctor discovered it one day 'by accident' when she came to look after my brother.

After that I had had to go to the cardiologist every year. He was a very impressive, silent specialist who ran his electrocardiograph and kept telling my mother, 'We'll wait until next year'.

I didn't know what he was waiting for, but when I was fifteen he said, 'It's time to operate, the heart is okay and she's fine, but she might not survive if she ever gives birth, and her heart might be tired when she reaches forty'.

I then went to a clinic in Marseilles for two weeks. It was the place where the first really successful heart transplant was done, on a man called Vitria who lived more than ten years with the heart of another person. I met a wonderful surgeon who had seven children and a huge motorbike. My mother was allowed to stay with me in the room. I met children with heart malformations who had to spend a month in a health centre with other children, before being hospitalised. They were terrified, seeing their friends going to the surgery room and never coming back. I saw in their eyes the fear and the pain of death.

I said to my mum the night before the surgery as we were watching the stars from the little balcony of our room, 'I'm not afraid of dying. You shouldn't worry for me if I die tomorrow. I just feel sorry to leave you, Papa, Henry and Michel. If I have to go, I will, but I really enjoy our family and my life'.

She was crying silently as I was feeling so calm and wise.

In the morning I was dressed in green to enter the surgery room. I remember the mask for the anaesthetic going over my face, and then I woke up in another room. I was full of tubes and there was machinery around me. My mother entered, dressed in green with a mask on her face. She was crying. I tried to smile, hiding the incredible physical pain I was feeling in my chest. I didn't know that it was possible to live with such pain. I thought that my heart would just stop completely under the pain. Then I felt a presence of light next to my right side, a sort of light and warmth, which reassured me and decreased my pain.

The surgeon told me later what he had done to me over four hours of surgery. Later still, through a technique of regression I learnt in the psychotherapy school, I was able to see it for myself. He had cut my chest and my sternum with a saw, then he had opened my ribs, using tools to keep them open while he took my heart out of my body. He connected me to a machine and then sewed the hole I had between the two upper cavities of my heart, before putting everything back in place. It wasn't surprising that I woke up in such pain!

He told me that because I was so relaxed, it was very easy to cut my heart. Apparently some people are so tense that it's difficult to operate. Seven days later I was back at school and nobody knew about my operation. I was only forbidden to use my moped for a month, until my sternum had knitted back together.

I had healed the trauma of my operation through different psychotherapy processes, but it was only when I went swimming with the Monkey Mia dolphins that I felt that something on the energy level in my heart was finally cleared.

I swam away from the beach with the dolphins, with the famous Holey Fin under my heart, swimming and sending sounds through my body with her sonar. Her baby swam with her, suckling underwater in my presence. I disappeared with them for hours, I couldn't be seen from the beach. As William was panicking on the shore I was having my heart operation finished — the dolphin way.

Such sound therapy, such high-tech surgery was absolutely revolutionary for me. I had spent seven years working on myself and learning different techniques to find, process and heal past traumas. Swimming with this pod of dolphins that were zapping me with their sonar system, I realised that I had a new heart. My heart *chakra* (centre of energy localised to the middle of the chest and different from the physical heart) was open and healed as never before.

I then realised that I had to swim back to the beach. The dolphins gave me the signal when they stopped, then sped away in a second out of my view. I was so far away from the coast that I couldn't see the beach. As I was swimming back, I suddenly realised that below me was a huge hammerhead shark (the bay is called Shark Bay for good reason).

As a diver, I have often met sharks like Port Jackson's and wobbegongs, which are just big fish. I dived in Tahiti once on a shark feed, but this was the first time I had met a shark while swimming on the surface. I had a flashback to the film *Jaws*, which traumatised so many people. I realised that I had the choice of being frightened or feeling protected by the dolphin energy I had just received. I chose the latter option, and swam back calmly to the beach. I found William alarmed and ready to send the rangers to find me. I told him my story, and we celebrated the dolphin healing.

DOUBTS DISPELLED

Sharing my dolphin adventures with William was very important in deepening our relationship. On the research side it was very reassuring to have an engineer from a select private school in England accepting my craziness about dolphins, and even becoming transformed by the experience himself. I always thought that I was my own guinea pig, and William was my first patient. He got rid of his fear of water through the first Dolphin Within program. Since then he had become more and more confident in the water, and started to be able to stay under water more than two minutes.

I felt even more reassured when I saw this smart engineer walking by himself on the beach (it can happen at Monkey Mia, between the busloads of tourists), and standing knee-deep in the water as six dolphins came straight towards him. He cuddled them and while I was still filming the encounter, he came straight to me and said, 'They want to play, *they told me*, they want us in the water to play.' (I don't remember any school of engineering teaching telepathy!)

So I dropped the video camera, grabbed my fins and mask and followed William into the water. We entered into a dance with four dolphins going from him to me, playing under water, imitating us imitating them. At one point I put my head on the sandy bottom and I saw a dolphin put his head down, just like me. We were dancing with them, touching them as they were asking for contact. It was like a wedding ceremony for both of us. It was like an initiation to their world of joy.

We came out unable to say anything, but with the same flame in our eyes. We both knew now about the dolphin energy. It was our common message, a mystery that we wanted to share with more. This removed any doubts I might have had about the dolphin energy. If William could experience it and tell me that they had communicated with him, I knew it would be possible to get the dolphin message to a broader audience, including the corporate world.

LOVE IN THE PACIFIC

We had left Monkey Mia in a state of bliss to get back to Sydney where William's office work kept him busy for a month before his annual holidays.

At that time we were still not making love, being faithful to my promise to be out of a relationship for a year. William was patient with me; I'm sure it wasn't easy for him! The deadline was March 1994. That month, I had planned to go back to Rapa Nui to see my brothers again. Our family reunions are always held on Rapa Nui rather than in France. A year earlier, I had asked all my friends if they wanted to come to Rapa Nui, as it's such a powerful place for self-transformation. William was the only one available and financially able to come.

So we had already planned to have a holiday together, and each time I spoke to my mum on the phone she asked if I would be staying with her, or if I wanted to be with my friend. She was very surprised that I was without a partner, for the first time in my life. Each time on the phone I reassured her, 'We're just friends. I'll spend the time with you, and stay in your bungalow. Yes, we need two beds.'

By the end of January 1995, I had to tell her that we would certainly need only one large bed and also a house of our own!

She was certainly disappointed not to share more time with me, but she really enjoyed meeting William, who managed to charm my brothers too, although none of them had long French conversations with him. The family feedback about William was, 'He's smart, polite and quiet, much better than your ex-husband, who was so talkative and so proud of himself!' (MBA complex.)

We had a great holiday, horse riding, snorkelling and scuba diving for two weeks. We saw the *moais* (statues) of Rapa Nui and felt the sacred space and energy. What was even more incredible was the way we made love for the first time, after being friends for years and deeply in love for five months. We had nearly made love in a Tahitian swimming pool under the stars, at the grand hotel we stayed in between our flight connections. However technically speaking, I can say that we really made love for the first time on Rapa Nui. I felt as if the whole energy of the volcanoes of the island were resonating with our own sexual energy. Reaching spiritual enlightenment through physical love became a reality that I could contemplate.

What we didn't know until later was that we managed to make a baby on that island. I was not surprised that a soul was attracted to the love energy of our coupling.

It is on Rapa Nui, or rather in the Rapa Nui waters, that William and I had our wedding. It was an underwater wedding, a simple dance and sacred commitment to each other in a hidden cave with a giant white coral reef as altar. Beautiful blue waters, no paper work and only the fish as witnesses!

THE MOTORBIKE ACCIDENT

We came back to Sydney from Rapa Nui on a Sunday night, and on the Monday as I rode my motorbike to work, I had an accident that had an profound influence on my life.

I was in Bondi Junction, an eastern suburb of Sydney, driving behind a taxi that indicated that he was stopping. As he stopped, I overtook him, and as I was just next to him, he suddenly turned to the right totally unaware of my presence. I ended up on the other side of the road while my motorbike was smashed on the ground. In shock, I stood up and wanted to leave to go to my training session. I then realised that I was bleeding, all over my left side. The taxi driver drove me to the nearest clinic and I collapsed in tears.

This accident, which happened on 16 March 1994, has had a huge impact on me. Despite the fact that I was, as I said before, a tomboy, that I went through heart surgery and many changes in my life, the motorbike accident was the worst event in my life. I was reduced to staying in bed at a time when I had just resigned from my job in order to create my own consulting company and have more time to dedicate to the dolphin research.

I was, within a few seconds, reduced to an invalid. I had worked all my life, even when I was studying. Suddenly I had no income and no way to work. My mother was still on Rapa Nui and I didn't want to worry her, nor my family in France.

However, I had William and the dolphins. William came and lived with me to look after me, and took me to the dolphins to bring me out of my depressed mood. Up until then, I had never felt real depression. Two aunts of mine had suffered from depression and one of them was successful in killing herself. I had known what depression meant, but I had never experienced it. Now I was feeling desperate, frightened and very fragile.

It was the first time in my life that my body didn't respond to my passion for life. I was feeling tired. I couldn't scuba dive any more, my left hand and left knee were cut everywhere and my lower back and neck were very painful. Nothing was broken but I could not really move without being in pain. The doctor's verdict was simple, 'You are disabled, just accept it, or go and see a psychiatrist to work out the grief'.

To add to the difficult situation, the taxi wasn't properly insured, so I had to struggle to find the name of the owner and his insurers. My motorbike was waiting to be repaired for a year, and even then the cost was not fully covered. My firm of solicitors, which was supposed to deal with the difficulties, was absolutely hopeless. Over three years I had seven different solicitors looking after my file and leaving the organisation one after the other. In March 1997, three years later, I finally had my first meeting with the other party, who offered a mediation conference in May. It then took six months for the respective solicitors to agree on a mediator. I could see how my own solicitor wanted to prolong the agony and go to court in order to earn more money. I had to fight to get the mediation, the win–win strategy, the dolphin way of dealing with conflict. Finally, on 26 August 1997, I had a full mediation with the insurance company and their solicitor to come up with an agreement.

I did not receive the full amount of compensation I was entitled to. However, I accepted to pay the price to be free of the system, free of the stress and pressure of such an inhuman process where solicitors who are supposed to support you are there to take advantage of you.

MISCARRIAGE WITH THE WHALES

To add to the difficult situation, I had discovered that I was pregnant after our trip to Rapa Nui. William having three children and me being so weak after the accident, the last thing I wanted was a baby. I had never been pregnant before, but William told me from his own experience that he was very good at making babies!

Instead of going to a hospital, I went to see the whales! William offered to pay for my ticket to Japan where I attended a conference on whales and dolphins. I left him promising to ask the whales to take away our baby. So I went to the ICERC (International Cetacean Education Research Centre) Conference in 1994, where I met for the first time Dr Horace Dobbs, Dr John Lilly, Jacques Mayol, Kamala Hope-Campbell and the global dolphin 'tribe'. We left Tokyo for the Ogasawara Islands, where it was possible to swim with dolphins and see whales.

On the whale watching day, I wanted to ask the whales to take my baby with them. We went out in many small boats, and their skippers chased the whales. I felt very sad. The whales were constantly swimming away. Eventually the boats turned to head for home, and my boat was the last to turn. As we did so, all the whales jumped out of the water, showing us their freedom and beauty. Such a spectacle put me into such a state of blessed shock that I had a spontaneous miscarriage.

I went swimming to clean my body and then I suffered in silence on the large boat that took us back to Tokyo. When I arrived in Sydney I went to my doctor. She listened to what I said and the tests confirmed that I was no longer pregnant but she didn't put the whales' intervention into my records.

I was weak for many weeks, but through more psychological exploration I could see that my body was in grief since the accident and the loss of the baby. I couldn't work; I was covered in scars, unable to walk properly, unable to stay in front of a computer for any length of time. I was quite depressed by the whole story, so I devoted all my time to the dolphin research, using myself as a guinea pig again.

I invited others to join me in my research on dolphin-assisted therapy, friends in the beginning, then other people interested in dolphins, some sick, depressed, or with 'normal' twentieth century neuroses. The case studies were collected, the pattern was becoming clearer. Something fascinating was happening during each weekend with the dolphins.

I spent a year doing full-time research, recovering from my motorbike accident and slowly starting to do more consulting work, as my health was getting better with more and more dolphin swims.

THE POWER OF A DOLPHIN THERAPIST

My treatment has been based on dolphin-assisted therapy. According to the insurance company I should have visited a psychiatrist, and had an operation for my neck, knee and my lower back.

I did visit the psychiatrist — twice. I came out of the room even more depressed than when I went in. The problem with psychiatrists is that they are people, and when you are depressed you have lost faith in human nature. The power of dolphins as therapists is that they are beyond human, they do not need to talk or ask questions, they just know. They have the power to look in your eye, make contact as a high intelligence and zap you with energy before going away.

I had a long eye contact with a wild dolphin, which stayed face to face with me, just in front of my mask. She stayed there looking into my eyes for what seemed like an eternity (time stops when a dolphin looks at you, another difference — the human psychiatrist works according to the clock!). As she looked at me I had the feeling she understood everything about me. She was acknowledging my pain and my beauty, and I was acknowledging her intelligence and presence.

The uniqueness of facing wild dolphins is that whatever state you are in — you can be depressed, have AIDS, be missing an arm, be mentally disabled, or whatever — they accept you as you are. You can just be — there is no word, no judgmental mind — only beingness, and you feel okay. They don't try to change you, to question you, to analyse you. They simply zap you with an unconditional love that transforms you.

So the only treatment I received following my motorbike accident was dolphin-assisted therapy and I can't claim against the insurance company for that. I can't say that I'm 100% fit. I've never been able to become a dive instructor, which was part of my vision and business plan. I can't say that I am a strong sailor as my neck and back hurt if I have to pull the sail hard. However, I'm no longer in a bed, and I'm no longer depressed.

According to the insurance people, I should have forgotten about my vision and my business plan. I should have gone back to a normal consulting job. With the stress and work pressure consultants go through in traditional consulting companies, I know that I would certainly not survive very long in such an environment!

But more importantly, I had a dream — to share more about a dolphin way to live. The dolphins have shown me another way, a smarter way to work. This 'dolphin way' was the 'raison d'être' behind the creation of ODB Consulting and the Dolphin Society. It is this vision that kept me going, that helped me to break through any obstacles.

So when the insurance company gave their verdict, saying that I should just forget about my vision, I wondered how many other people have lost their dream and given up when facing such a system.

5

THE DOLPHIN SOCIETY IS BORN

Perhaps the time has come to formulate a moral code which would govern our relations with the great cetaceans of the sea as well as with those on dry land. That this will come to pass is our greatest wish. If human civilisation is going to invade the waters of the earth, then let it be first of all to carry a message of respect, respect for all life.

Jacques-Yves Cousteau (1910–97)

William and I became aware that it was important to create an organisation, separate from our consulting company, which could bring together people who want to learn more about dolphins.

A couple of different organisations had tried to attract us, because they could see the potential of our project and the possibility of attracting dolphins to places where they wanted to create centres. However, we did not want to sell our vision for any commercial venture. It felt very important to preserve our values more than our bank account, to have freedom to move in whatever direction the dolphins took us. We decided to create the Dolphin Society.

Starting our own company was already a challenge, but creating a non-profit organisation at the same time was quite crazy. Nevertheless, that is what we did!

AN OUTLINE OF THE SOCIETY

The Dolphin Society is an Australian-based, non-profit research foundation dedicated to exploring the effects on humans of interaction with dolphins, facilitating a process of discovering the 'Dolphin Within'. The Society was established to research the effects on humans of interaction with dolphins. These effects can be seen on various levels — physiological, psychological and spiritual — and suggest that new methods of healing and self-development can be developed through a knowledge of how they work. The Society's activities include:

1. Developing and undertaking a program of research into the effects on

people of interaction with dolphins. Spreading an awareness of these effects by publicising the results of the research, and possible applications thereof.

2. Establishing Dolphin Therapy Centres where the results of the research can be applied.

3. Encouraging conservation of dolphin habitats and in particular facilitating the return of dolphins to Sydney Harbour by 2000.

The first objective is being realised through the Dolphin Within program. It is the research program centred on two-day sailing trips where participants with different conditions (depression, disabilities, etc.) make contact with dolphins in the wild and experience the dolphins' environment, through snorkelling and scuba diving. Participants undergo physiological and psychological testing using techniques developed to monitor the effects of dolphin contact. They are also involved in follow-up individual and group sessions.

The aim is to share the results of the research, as they become available, through appropriate means including books (like this one) electronic communications, multimedia, the news media, film, and specialist publications. In this respect the Society's Internet home page attracts substantial interest.

The second objective is to establish Dolphin Therapy Centres where the results of the research can be applied, without use of real dolphins. This will enable greater numbers of people to experience the therapeutic effects of dolphin encounters without posing any threat to the dolphins and their fragile and threatened environment. Such centres will accommodate natural pools in which the experience of meeting dolphins in the sea will be artificially recreated. People will go swimming, snorkelling and scuba diving while prerecorded dolphin sounds and images will be transmitted through the water. This combination of virtual reality with the physical environment is expected to provide a memorable and therapeutic experience.

The third objective is realised by cleaning Sydney Harbour and by promoting a more responsible attitude among people involved in interactions with the ocean and the environment. Behind that project is a vision to create Best Practices for harbour management including stormwater management as the only pollution to the marine environment (apart from vessels) comes from the land.

To further achieve these aims the Society forms links with like-minded organisations around the world, to create a forum where matters of dolphin-human interaction on all levels — historical, mythological, scientific, psychological and spiritual — can be shared with the global community.

THE POD

When we created the Society we wanted to include in the pod, the committee, people with wide talents and to combine scientists, environmentalists and artists.

We first invited Peter Shenstone, whom I had met three years earlier in the Blue Mountains. Peter was known worldwide in dolphin circles for his work in spreading the *Legend of the Golden Dolphin*, a collection of stories that show how dolphins have interacted with humans at critical times in history, almost always before a flowering of civilisation.

Fifteen years ago, Peter was a successful marketing consultant. Following his dolphin experience, he left the business world to travel widely, sharing the Legend of the Golden Dolphin. During that time he organised a trip to Monkey Mia, travelling across Australia by bus with artists, musicians and children to produce a film of the dolphins. To listen to Peter is to vibrate at dolphin frequencies. He has the art of telling stories that encapsulate and preserve both the authenticity of the legend and the beauty of the experience.

When we approached him again, Peter was Chairman of Planet Ark Australia, an environmental agency whose purpose is to make us aware of our personal impact on the natural world, and of the inextricable link between the wellbeing of the planet and human health.

PLANET ARK

Planet Ark Environmental Foundation is a new-paradigm environmental change agency that defines itself by what it is for rather, than what it is against. It is non-political and non-confrontational. Its primary mission is environmental education presented in an engaging and entertaining way, to show people and organisations what they can do to help save the planet in their day-to-day lives at home, at work, and at play.

Planet Ark operates as an environmental agency under the motto 'where conservation means business', underlining a commitment to environmental solutions that are solidly rooted in marketplace viability.

• *Mass media and celebrity support*
Planet Ark dispenses environmental good news stories and tips, presented by celebrity supporters, and broadcast widely through strong long-term media alliances. On the Channel Seven television network, for example, around 200 Planet Ark 'Save the Planet' community service ads have been produced and aired in prime time over the last

five years. The latest series is also aired on the regional Prime television network.

Under the umbrella of 'Save the Planet' awareness, Planet Ark runs a series of annual campaigns such as National Worm Week, National Tree Day, and National Recycling Week.

Recycling is the one environmental action that almost everyone can take part in.

• Stores and environmental products

Planet Ark is establishing a network of stores around Australia and the rest of the world. These stores sell a full range of environmentally friendly products, including: white goods (fridges and washing machines); natural paints and varnishes; personal and health care products; cleaning products: and water and energy saving products.

Planet Ark environmentally safe cleaning products (laundry powder and dishwashing liquid) do not use any dangerous or toxic substances, are not tested on animals and yet provide a high standard of cleaning. After using these products, the grey water can safely be re-used on gardens. These products are also sold through Coles supermarkets.

Our 'non-contaminated' psychologist was Dr Idir Bahamid, a friend and management consultant partner who didn't know anything about dolphins. He is a psychologist working in corporate training and development.

Our dolphin specialist was Dr Peter Corkeron, a veterinary scientist working first for Sydney University, and then for James Cook University. He was one of Australia's foremost authorities on whales and dolphins. He brings to the Society a wealth of knowledge and experience in working with dolphins in the wild. Peter has run cetacean research projects in Hervey Bay, Moreton Bay and elsewhere around Australia, as well as travelling overseas and to Antarctica.

It was very important for us to have artists in the Society. This happened when we met Howie Cooke. Howie is a New Zealander who is well known for his work in campaigning for whale and dolphin conservation in the Pacific over the last twenty years. He is a highly talented artist whose work has inspired many people; Greenpeace adopted one of his many whale paintings for a design to commemorate the Southern Ocean Whale Sanctuary.

Meeting Howie and hearing him talk about dolphins and whales is quite an experience. Seeing his paintings is something else! Entering his Bondi flat is like entering the world of the people of the sea. There are incredible dolphin and whale paintings all over the walls, and you can feel the energy of the whales and dolphins infiltrating your blood. Howie painted our minibus, and helped us to create our first T-shirt and postcard.

The first night we met, Howie shared his experience.

> I've been swimming in and under the sea, and drawing and painting since I was knee high to a grasshopper. School channelled me into the sciences and I ended up working in plant hormone and pesticide research — but I escaped! ... ultimately to an island and during that time [beginning in 1976] I made a powerful emotional and spiritual connection with the whales which led me into my life of painting.
>
> Right from the first big whale canvas [of a humpback] I was inspired by dolphins and they gave me very real encouragement and direction. Their inspiration has stayed with me.

The day Howie came to our flat two years later to proofread this part of the book, six humpback whales stayed an hour in our bay, breaching in front of our eyes.

HOWIE'S DOLPHIN WITHIN EXPERIENCE

Howie offered straight away to paint our minibus and we invited him to come and see the dolphins. That weekend we had Brendan Macpherson (Elle's brother) and his friend Justin. Howie invited some friends from Chinatown, Lee Leng from the famous Bodhi's restaurant, and her daughter, Heaven (Heaven Lee!) As we were driving back to Sydney, Howie wrote the following words that recaptured beautifully the atmosphere of that weekend.

> Dolphins. Circles and spirals. A drive in the cetacean wagon with nuances. A rendezvous with les gens de la mer. Mermaids and mermen-to-be. Nelson Bay a long way from Trafalgar Square. *Orca.* A spectacular sunset incinerating the clouds and we see a beautiful burning angel, and the big masts moaning in the wind down the jetty. Ethereal music for a full moon...
>
> Sleeping on water (ZZZ/H$_2$O). Orquatic dreams. Lee Leng and Heaven on board. Imagine travelling to dolphins with Heaven on board! Brendan Justin time. Weigh anchor and decide to take it. Itching to raise the sails. They look like folded butterfly wings or lingerie waiting to be hoisted out of a department store. Throw anchor over the side but decide to keep it. Check our licences to see if they're current. Do current swim. Dolphins challenge us to a race, but cheat like crazy. Everyone gets wet and thank the dolphins for such a great idea.
>
> Try throwing the anchor away again, but decide to keep the boat. Swim over grassy bed. Lots of people sleeping on it ... Heaven and I meet a tiny stingray and love the way he/she is more ray than sting. Olivia and William sur la plage aussi and we flow swim amongst the kelp and street

urchins. I'm sorry? Oh, yes, sea urchins. Flatheads everywhere. They must have trouble with the pressure. Heaven is an angel in the water. We ask the anchor to come on board. Sail towards the sun — but it keeps its distance, turning to syrup on the horizon. We slide into a bay and dolphins chase us out (in their very subtle way!)

Beautiful sea eagle swooping over two dolphins as they delve along the forest edge. Go back into the bay when the dolphins aren't looking. The anchor dives off the boat and we all got caught again by its 'last one in is a dirty rat' trick. Dang. Go ashore with food, in the other boat *Orcette*, who has been following us faithfully. Big fire and big mosquitos. The night was magical with a certain moustique. The puns were almost intolerable, but the food was great. Guitar dessert. 'Blue guitar notes vie with the rustling green, while animals speaking in many tongues are sometimes never heard, sometimes never seen' (Tonga, 1979). Squid black sky gives way to the mother of all pearls. The moon! Rising over our leafy heads. Polar-eyes'd light and a party boat full of rock classics (but it still floated!)

Moon magic weaving threads around Brendan and Heaven. Olivia and William nestled up near the pointy end. Snogging. Morning arrives on time and as usual I'm not quite punctual — but we get away. The anchor comes too. Head to a rendez-Jim, to learn Tuba. Bit hard on the ears so Lee-Leng teaches me how to appreciate the sunlit sand and little sprats. She finds her flippers in this new world. Find myself away in a world of octopus, trumpet fish, wrasse luderick (a type of poem). Find a great rock with a single moorish idol, a massive moray — very interesting how the one crevasse was occupied by a — where is my fish book — ah yes, that's right, an eastern wirrah as well. Around the back a large wobbegong shark lay sleeping. Along the way a green turtle swimming irregularly, a folded metal clip thing caught on its flipper. My heart sighed sadly.

Imagine a world where we could swim straight to our friends and help them and they had no reason to fear us. I turned back not wishing to upset the beautiful turtle. On the way back some old wives caught my eye. I guess I'm not as young as I used to be! What a silly name for such unique fish — there ought to be stonefish called 'old husbands', perhaps. Little sand toads swimming with a little cuttlefish. They seemed very happy together. The cuttlefish suddenly made like a rock, changing its whole body colour and skin texture, crouching stoically next a similar-sized rock, mimicking its shape.

This one little event really touched me. It sitting there immobile as a statue, a beautiful vulnerable little buddha of the sea, symbolising the precious and delicate nature of the ocean world. I wanted to kiss this cuttlefish! To reach out and say 'I want you to be a happy little cuttlefish and I love you.' I left the water pondering how the love and inspiration the whale and dolphins show us is sometimes given to us by their companions in the sea ...

As we arrived back in Sydney, I wondered when Howie would have his Dolphin Within experience. After all, he had had so many encounters with dolphins and whales in his life; could anything really be new to him? But I should not have worried. Howie did indeed have a Dolphin Within experience the following day, when I introduced him to my lover.

WILDERNESS THERAPY WITH BLUEY

Howie stayed the night with us in our unit and the next morning we all went swimming with my lover, the blue groper. Howie couldn't stay in the water long enough! And the magic happened; two old souls met!

Since then he has visited the groper many times, and they have become very close. He named him Bluey. Howie told me that he misses him when he spends time away from him.

Bluey is a special fish. I started interacting with him when I first moved to Clovelly. I was introduced to him in 1990 by John Rowe, a diver friend. Since then I go and swim with Bluey every morning. I confess that I give him a sea snail each day as a present. I never feed dolphins, because their love is unconditional. However Bluey is not a dolphin.

As his name indicates, Bluey is a fantastic blue colour. I love seeing him underwater. I had explored pet therapy with my dog in France when I was twenty; she was a beautiful female Alsatian who loved the sea as much as I do.

I discovered wilderness therapy with Bluey. When I left my work and my partner, my only relationship with a male was with Bluey. I used to call him my lover. I realised how therapeutic it was for me to go and swim with him every morning, to receive his love.

I observed that this therapy was also working on John, the diver who first introduced me to Bluey. John is a typical Australian man, in his late forties, strong and not really delicate. He did teach me, however, to approach Bluey delicately and not to rush up after him. I remember one morning, as we were both snorkelling with Bluey, John came up to the surface with wide eyes, saying, 'He loves me!'

His heart was so open it was quite amazing and I thought, 'If that fish can open a heart like that, what a powerful process!'

Since then I have introduced Bluey to many friends and Howie has organised many swims for his friends. They are all amazed by Bluey's colour and gentleness. Howie and I also started to interact with other fish: there is Mascara, another blue groper with the classic yellow scribble lines around his eyes, Miss Pignose and Goldie, Bluey's favourite female companions who are still quite shy.

One day, I was taking a photo of Bluey while I was giving him some food and I forgot to withdraw my finger because I was focusing the camera with my other hand. My whole finger disappeared into his mouth. But Bluey has no teeth, only powerful lips that vacuum virtually anything. I got my finger back from this love bite. I try not to touch Bluey. It's difficult because his blue is very attractive but I try to respect his space. I prefer when he comes and touches me. I do the same with the dolphins; I prefer to let them initiate the touch.

Bluey sometimes disappears for days at a time, usually when it is stormy. I suppose it's because he could be easily bruised on the rocks, and also because the bay gets very polluted when the storm water flows. When it happens, I always have Howie on the phone checking if I have seen Bluey while John asks me the same question when we meet on the beach. I am always touched to see how this fish has entered the hearts of these two very different men. The whole Clovelly community seems to ask each other every morning, 'Have you see the blue groper?'

One Saturday morning, after ten days with no sign of Bluey, John told me that he was feeling sad, but he was trying to prepare himself for the worst, knowing that Bluey is at least twenty years old. Then we jumped in, I called the fish with my high-pitched sound, he appeared, and we all played happily, a little celebration of life.

AN OCEANIC RESERVE

I play with all the fish in the bay, in a kind of aquatic reserve where they come. They follow me around like pilot fish. They come right up to my mask, looking at me, Bluey included.

Every day more and more fish come to play with us under water. It amazes me how quickly they become happy to play with people when we stop killing them. I'd love to take fishermen snorkelling, feeding the fish by hand to experience the beauty of the exchange. I'm sure some would stop killing them.

The little oceanic reserve we have created here is the beginnings of what we see as a Dolphin Therapy Centre. We want to create a place where anyone can come and swim, snorkel and interact with the fish and underwater life, listening to dolphin sounds underwater. If at some stage dolphins want to join in, they would be free to do so, but the healing effect would be almost as powerful without them. Such a place would be a sanctuary for people to experience the ocean.

We still have a long way to go in terms of pollution and water waste. In Clovelly for example, as soon as it rains the bay becomes very toxic and we can't swim for days until everything is cleaned away by the sea. The storm water goes directly into the sea, bringing all the rubbish and cigarette butts that destroy the marine life.

In 1996, the local council developed a management plan for Clovelly Bay. I went to the public meeting organised by the consultants, where the community was invited to present their concerns and ideas. I spoke about the storm water, the cigarette butts and the fishing issues, especially the spear fishing which puts Bluey the groper in so much danger. Over the years, I have often discovered him with a big wound from a fisherman's spear. He seems to recover each time, but it takes weeks of healing. I also mentioned the fact that each time the council cleans the steps that lead into the water with chlorine, I find dead fish floating in the bay. I will always remember the morning I arrived to find all 'my' fish, my friends, floating belly up in the chlorine pond.

When I received the draft of the management plan. I was very happy to read that the consultants recommend banning fishing in the bay, and to find an alternative to chlorine for cleaning the steps. However in the small print it appears that the fishing ban is proposed, not to preserve the fish, but because lost hooks are dangerous for swimmers, and also because with the use of chlorine the fish may be too toxic for human consumption!

I'm amazed how these things are always viewed from a limited, human perspective. It's always about protecting the humans that we create rules or policies. The ban was never adopted, too risky to offend the fishermen.

It was this kind of limited thinking that has made it so important for us to establish a declaration of the rights of the people of the sea (the whales, dolphins and porpoises), which we hope one day will include all marine species, indeed all life on earth.

In the meantime, each time I see a fisherman in Clovelly Bay, I go and talk to him (I haven't seen yet a fisherwoman). One early morning, I saw a young guy fishing and gently I approached him and asked:

'Do you know this bay?'

'Not particularly.'

'In this bay, the fish have names and the people go and play with them. They are our friends. I am going now to meet them and I feel sad that you are going to kill them. Have you ever snorkelled? If you want to try, I can lend you my mask, it is beautiful down there.'

He was looking at me with big eyes of surprise and then he asked me: 'What are their names?'

'The big blue groper is Bluey, then you have Mascara, Pig Nose, and also hundred of small ones which are also part of the family. There is no ban on fishing in this bay, if you want to stay.'

'No I did not know, thank you, I also snorkel and love seeing the fish, I can go and fish somewhere else.'

And he took his pushbike and left. I went to see my friends.

The dialogue is not always so easy but this encounter was confirming the importance of taking a risk to defend my friends' lives. I was not fighting; I was sharing my personal experience, talking from heart to heart.

ANTI-NUCLEAR TEST DEMONSTRATION

Howie's art and activism are a very valuable energy for the Dolphin Society. At the time of the French decision to resume nuclear tests in the South Pacific, Howie transformed our minibus, 'the bubble', to be part of the demonstration march to the French Embassy. We thought that it was very important for us to represent the dolphins and whales. After all, they are one of the important stakeholders in the oceans, far more than us humans, and we never stop to think what their point of view might be in terms of nuclear tests, bombs in the ocean.

We brought the minibus but the police stopped us joining the march, so we parked it in a strategic position and joined the demonstration on foot. I walked along holding an inflatable dolphin over my head. The response of the crowd was beautiful. People opened the way for the dolphin. I remember seeing a little boy sitting on his father shoulders, as I was sitting on William's shoulders. He was holding a placard that he dropped straight away to hold the dolphin.

As the crowd opened the way for me and the dolphin, I found myself facing Senator Bob Brown, an Australian environmentalist and politician. He was addressing the crowd and the news cameras from the stairs in front of the French Embassy. At one point he said in a very loud and dramatic voice, 'We are talking in the name of the Australians, we are talking in the name of the Tahitians', and then he looked at the dolphin who was facing him right in the eyes, and he added, 'We are talking in the name of all species!'

The dolphin nodded his nose to approve the speech while the whole crowd burst into applause. Later people came to me to thank me for the dolphin presence.

DECLARATION OF RIGHTS

On 3 March 1996, exactly a year after meeting Howie, the Dolphin Society was able to bring into reality his dream of having a Declaration of Rights for Cetaceans.

Universal Declaration of Marine Mammal Rights
Charter One: Cetaceans (Whales, Dolphins and Porpoises)

In recognition of the special relationship that exists between cetaceans and humans, this Charter seeks the immediate extension of the *Universal Declaration of Human Rights* (United Nations, 1948) to include whales, dolphins and porpoises.

Whales, dolphins and porpoises, the 'People of the Sea' — large-brained, intelligent and highly socialised — have an ancient and unblemished history of offering us, the people of the land, only joyful friendship, compassion and good humour, despite our continual transgressions against them and their environment.

In extending the concept of the *Universal Declaration of Human Rights* to them, it should be noted that Cetacean Rights are not new — we have not invented them. We cannot give them to cetaceans because they are theirs already — they are their inheritance from birth. We can only re-declare them, and echo the fact that they belong to the cetaceans and that we, the humans, have many times robbed them of their rightful heritage.

1. All whales, dolphins and porpoises are born free and equal in dignity and rights. They are endowed with reason and conscience and act towards one another in a spirit of brotherhood.
2. Every whale, dolphin and porpoise is entitled to all the rights and freedom set forth in this Declaration, without distinction of any kind such as species, sex or other status.
3. Every whale, dolphin and porpoise has the right to life, liberty and security of person.
4. No whale, dolphin or porpoise shall be held in slavery or servitude; slavery and the slave trade shall be prohibited in all their forms.
5. No whale, dolphin or porpoise shall be subjected to misfortune or to cruel, inhuman or degrading treatment or punishment.
6. No whale, dolphin or porpoise shall be subjected to arbitrary arrest, detention or exile.
7. Every whale, dolphin and porpoise has the right to freedom of movement and residence in the sea and the right to return unhindered to its home territory.
8. Every whale, dolphin and porpoise has the right to freedom of peaceful assembly and association.
9. Every cetacean has the right to a clean environment for the health and wellbeing of self and family and the right to the bounty of the ocean, i.e. food.
10. Nothing in this Declaration may be interpreted as implying for any State, group or person any right to engage in any activity or to perform any act aimed at the destruction of any of the rights and freedoms set forth herein.

DOLPHIN CONCERT ON SYDNEY HARBOUR

We launched the Declaration at a concert we had organised on Sydney Harbour. Overcome with joy and a throat infection Howie was speechless, but well-known musician Ken Davis played his heart out. William added song and guitar. We collected 100 signatures straight away. William put the charter on the Internet, while I sent it to France, South Africa and Rapa Nui.

We connected with Ken Davis through true dolphinicity. Ken saw our Internet site just before Christmas 1995, and sent us an e-mail to say hello. William and I were meditating for two weeks so we didn't answer. Early in January, we had our first 1996 trip organised when Sabrina, one of the participants, called to say that she was stuck in Queensland because of a tropical cyclone, and wouldn't be able to join us. I thought about calling someone from our long waiting list when William said with a very sure voice, 'You don't need to, someone's going to call tomorrow'.

When I came home from a client meeting the following day, William said, 'Guess what! Ken Davis called to see if he could come and meet the dolphins. I said, "Come tomorrow, if you want", and he's coming!'

That weekend with Ken was a musical trip. I brought a keyboard as usual, and Ken played music to the dolphins. He also fell in love with William's guitar.

Following the weekend, Ken wrote a new dolphin music album: *Dolphin Magic*. Over the weekend, Ken had the idea to organise a concert afloat on Sydney Harbour, and within six weeks we had made all the arrangements. On the day, which was also *Clean Up Australia Day,* we had glorious weather and over 100 people on the boat. The concert was a great success (as was the clean-up of the beach!).

Later, Ken and I discovered that we share the same birthday. Dolphinicity strikes again!

THE DOLPHIN EVENINGS

We run our Dolphin Within research trips every second weekend, and once a month we meet for a dolphin evening. It is important for us to provide a night for dolphin people to meet. We have shared such deep experiences together and created strong links, and it's also a way for people to keep in contact with the research through the years.

During each trip we create a dolphin 'pod', in which people start to interact with unconditional love. We then put the pods together, and we have the Dolphin Society, which can start to make a difference in the world.

The dolphin evening is also open for people who want to know more about us, or people who are about to join us on an expedition. Anyone can join to come and talk about dolphins, and enjoy a vegetarian meal. Scientists, philosophers and artists often meet together to learn from each other.

One night, Peter Shenstone shared with the group the Legend of the Golden Dolphin: how dolphins always come at different points in history to help us humans to make it through the transition phase. The way Peter shared the legend was unbelievable. At one point he mentioned the importance of singing and music.

I asked Ruth, who was with us on the boat the weekend before, to share her experience. She told how William started singing in Latin, and the dolphins came straight away.

Peter picked up the word 'Latin', and explained that dolphins use sonic communication, sending information through a vibration and receiving information as a hologram. One of the best conductors for receiving holographic information is liquid, which is what dolphins have in their front head or melons.

Peter continued, 'A friend told me that ancient languages have kept the sonic formula which modern ones have lost. That would explain why Sanskrit and Latin songs attract the dolphins. The power of the word.'

Dawn Ferguson, who was visiting from the United States after working with dolphins in the Bahamas, confirmed that when she meditates using Sanskrit words, the dolphins come. Dawn then shared another story, 'I was playing guitar by the pool with the dolphins, thinking how terrible it was that we can't communicate. A dolphin came and looked at me, put her nose on the guitar and moved it along the strings. Clearly she had caught my thought and was answering, "We can communicate through music".'

Peter told us of another instance in Monkey Mia, where one person started dancing on the beach and a dolphin came and danced in front of him. A second person joined, followed by a second dolphin, then a third person was followed by third dolphin. Dolphinicity again!

At another dolphin evening, Philip, a close friend of William, a great chef with an international reputation, stood up and expressed to the group his dream of leaving his job and opening a café where the dolphin people could come and meet, enjoying a great vegetarian food. The dolphin energy was really with him as he was talking. His heart was open and his eyes were sparkling. Within six weeks, Philip had managed to find a café in the centre of Sydney, where, exactly as he said, the dolphin people could meet monthly. Philip joined the Dolphin Society Committee in 1996.

DOLPHIN WITHIN PRESENTATIONS

Through experiences like Philip's, it became clearer to William and me that it was possible to bring the dolphin energy wherever we wanted to. So we started to give presentations, talks to any organisation that wanted to know more about dolphins.

We gave our first Dolphin Within presentation for an organisation called the Spirit of Learning. It was a great experience. We were very relaxed in our dolphin energy. William introduced me and said how much I inspire him. I was surprised and touched by his words.

I started talking, like a flow, the joy of sharing our dolphin stories. Estelle Myers' film *Dreams of Dolphins Dancing* had a strong impact — the participants stared transfixed at the screen. William did a great brainstorming session using the white board, and we ran a dolphin meditation session.

The sharing time was quite moving. One participant said that the workshop gave her ways to solve a conflict in their life: 'There is a problem at work with one staff member. During the relaxation I got a message from the dolphins telling me how to handle the conflict. I need to get closer to the lady, even to touch her to put her in my energy.'

Another lady was crying, releasing some emotional pain.

We were surprised ourselves at the power of the process we had designed for a presentation of less than two hours. We realised how strong the dolphin energy was, and how easy it is for us to bring it anywhere, even to the top of the Queen Victoria Building in the centre of Sydney.

We started to do more presentations like that to spread the word. We were soon invited to different conferences around the world. In June 1996 we went to a conference in London and Amsterdam organised by our famous friend Dr Horace Dobbs.

It was moving to meet the heroes of Horace's books and films, such as Bill Bowell, who swam with dolphins to recover from depression, Jemima Biggs (anorexia) and the beautiful Lilo Slumiok-Muller (cancer).

The most moving experience of all was with Eve Hanf-Enos, a highly intelligent young woman who suffers from autism. Her spirit pervaded the room as she communicated to us via her little computer. As William said, 'One wonders who needs healing when you hear Eve's poems and insights'.

Konoe and Kokyo Ishizaki from the Qi Dolphin Healing Centre in Japan, were there to explain, through Shizuko's translation, the way they practise healing in their temple in Kyoto.

It was also great to meet Amanda Cochrane, the co-writer of *Dolphins and their Power to Heal*, who wants our research results to help update her book.

We gave a multimedia presentation, compiled by William, with films and photos of our trips, the brain research, Howie's paintings and cartoons and the Internet page, to give them an idea of what we do in Australia. It was very rewarding to have people come up at the end to thank us for having inspired them. Many people wanted to come and join us in Australia.

In 1997 we were invited as speakers at the 6th International Dolphin and Whale Conference organised by ICERC in Hervey Bay, Queensland, a moving reunion of the dolphin people from all over the world.

6

DOLPHIN WITHIN PATTERNS

I suspect that whales and dolphins quite naturally go in the directions we call spiritual, in that they get into meditative states quite simply and easily. If you go into the sea yourself, with snorkel and facemask and warm water, you can find that dimension in yourself quite easily. Free floating is entrancing ... Now if you combine snorkelling and scuba with a spiritual trip with the right people, you could make the transition to understanding the dolphins and the whales very rapidly.

Dr John Lilly ★

IT'S ABOUT EXPERIENCING, NOT BELIEVING

I see each Dolphin Within program as a way to create a human pod where people learn the dolphin way of living. William and I never say anything to the people on the yacht about our own experiences. We never explain the deep healing processes we have been through ourselves. At the beginning of each adventure I always simply say, 'Our purpose is to create a safe space for the dolphins and humans to interact, all of us on the yacht are researchers or students of the Dolphin School. Observe what is happening for yourself, the dolphins and others. Try to reflect upon your Dolphin Within experience and record your observations by writing, drawing, talking to the video camera. Our approach is more about learning from the dolphins than trying to touch them. Learning to live in their environment and to be dolphins ourselves on the yacht, in terms of teamwork, support, freedom and fun'.

We always emphasise the importance of not believing in anything but just 1) experiencing the dolphins, 2) reflecting to formulate a personal knowledge and 3) sharing and looking for patterns. Each weekend brings four or five people together and even if it isn't a large number, slowly, we built up an important knowledge bank and a society of people who can make a difference in their lives and on the planet.

At the end of each Sunday night, as we unload the gear from the minibus

★ Lilly is regarded by many as the father of dolphin research.

at midnight after the three-hour drive home to Sydney, William and I feel fulfilled and contented at achieving our mission. We know that we make a difference in the lives of four people each weekend with the dolphins. Recalling the parting hugs, and the 'thank you, thank you very much. I really feel like a different person' makes us feel honoured to serve the dolphin energy and privileged to be the instruments of such a powerful form of human transformation.

Through the expeditions we started to identify some clear 'Dolphin Within Patterns'.

Each individual case we describe is typical of at least 10 to 15 people who have made similar observations. I have chosen the most representative stories to relate; bear in mind that each individual's process could be a book in itself. Each trip is an incredible adventure into human transformation. We have had more than 60 expeditions, more than 240 people, many books to write. Each expedition is part of a longer process, each phase of which brings learning for us all.

The Dolphin Within program is not only a two-day program; the process starts as soon as people contact us and commit themselves to come to meet the dolphins. People often report having dreams of dolphins before the actual trip. Months, years later, they still remember their experience; it still affects their lives. The following stories are detailed, because the program is not simply about jumping in the water with dolphins. It is about being with a human being, understanding their whole journey and co-creating with the dolphins a therapy, healing and self-development process.

In he following text, each time you see the dolphin logo it means that another Dolphin Within Pattern is described.

 FREE FROM FEAR OF THE SEA

Prue, a Melbourne nurse who was afraid of water, jumped in as soon as she saw the dolphins. She later wrote the following in her journal:

> I have always been terrified of interacting by myself in the sea. I am not familiar with it at all. So as soon as the dolphins arrived, the first night when we were all singing together, tears streamed from my eyes. I was overcome with emotion. The next morning I was alone, it was the first step, but I still didn't feel at ease. The dolphins were close, we jumped in. I didn't give it a second thought. I was in there interacting with them, listening to them chatting. It wasn't until the three of us were on the back of the dinghy that I thought: 'Aargh, what am I doing?'
>
> Back on the boat, I read my pre-swim notes. My body had felt blocked,

especially at the fingers, the energy could not break there. Now I feel vital, alive like the sea, almost cleansed. The adrenalin and vitality and the work of conquering my fear of the ocean had exhausted me, and I felt into a tranquil sleep.

Next step, scuba-diving, the fear of fears. Strange, I could have backed out but I didn't. Initially I was absolutely mortified. I clutched Jim the dive instructor's hand. Gradually, I relaxed into the relaxing ways of underwater. The beauty, the peace, the feeling of being at one. Jim's grip got lighter until our fingertips barely touched. I had done it; I had dived. The most incredible experience. On our ascent, dolphins were very close, almost as if to say: 'Well done, Prue, we knew you could do it.' I had re-connected with myself. It's been a long time lost. I'm glad I found me. I feel mellow and at ease. I have found my dolphin within.

A week after the program, she passed her scuba diving certificate and has being diving since then.

Prue's experience shows how the Dolphin Within program is ideal for anyone who is frightened of water. William was the first guinea pig, and since then we have received many people scared of the sea, some due to accidents they don't remember, or deeply felt phobias. Through the program they always end up in the water and many, like Prue, discover scuba diving. We also have many people who can't swim enjoy the water by floating with a wet suit, mask and snorkel. We have many cases of people who couldn't swim who went scuba diving. These cases confirm our hypothesis that the dolphins create a learning environment that fosters people's feelings of safety, security and peace and breakthrough.

 FREE FROM GRIEF

I invited Roger, a blind friend, to join a Dolphin Within expedition. As Roger was in a taxi, explaining that he was going to swim with dolphins, the taxi-driver said: 'I know a television producer who might be interested in your trip.'

We ended up with a very special trip on 14–15 January 1995, with Roger and Robyn, Scott and Philip from Channel Nine's *The Today Show*. Geoff from the Animal Ethics Committee was also on board, visiting to check that we were respecting the dolphins.

We had no idea what perspective the television film would be made from. We were advised to be on our guard with TV and the media, to ask them if we could review the film before they put it on TV. As usual, we trusted the process, giving them the Dolphin Within experience without trying to convince, just showing them the truth of what we do and letting them get their own learning and draw their own conclusions. We had no fear, only trust, and we received a beautiful film as a gift, a short piece that explains and totally respects the work we do, with no sensationalism.

The weather that weekend was fantastic, and as soon as we left the port, the dolphins surrounded the boat, taking everyone by surprise. Roger quickly got used to the boat and how to get into the water. He asked us to describe each obstacle or piece of equipment he was using: the back of the boat, the ladder, the rope, the buoy and the dinghy.

Filming dolphins is an art. You never know where they will come out of the water, and the cameraman wasn't always ready for them. I thought that in the future if we want to make our own professional film, we would need to let the film crew interact with the dolphins for a week or more before they could operate with intuition and connect with them.

Seeing from within

At the beginning of the trip, Roger was very excited. He was the star on board, talking a lot, making jokes. The second day was quite different. After the swim he went into a state of calmness and silence, the words he used were: 'I'm in a contemplative state'.

This was very different to the usual image he presented to the world, always full of life and very talkative. He just went inside, wanted to be by himself. I observed him from a distance, giving him some space.

At one point in his meditative stage he asked: 'Could the dolphin come to the bow?'

He went to the bow and started calling them by tapping on the boat. He asked Philip, the cameraman, if the dolphins were there. As Philip was saying no, two dolphins jumped in front of Roger. He tapped the bow again and they came under his hand. I was filming the scene. I could see he had made a connection with them. He was initiated to their world. He was starting to see them with his inner eye.

Dolphins use their sonar system to detect any presence. It is a much more sophisticated system than our physical eyes. Dolphins can send a sound and receive a reflection back, which they translate in their melon, a wax-filled sac which somehow projects a holographic picture for them, a 3D picture which provides information about the outside and inside of the object. Research has also shown that they can pick up people's thoughts and emotions.

Observing Roger made me wonder: could humans develop such a sensory system? Could blind people be even more attuned to such an organ? Isn't this what eastern philosophy calls the Third Eye? Some of us know what it is to 'tune in' to a person. How far can we develop our own sonar system?

Emotional release

Roger went back to his contemplative state and I stayed with him, caring for him from a distance. The rest of the crew was talking in the cockpit, unaware of what was happening. I knew that something deep was happening for Roger, I could feel it from a distance. 'Tuning in' to him, I knew he was crying. I left him the space to go through his emotional release. Then I sat down beside him: 'You shouldn't be surprised if you feel a little bit bizarre emotionally today and in the following days, because the dolphin effect is a process and it lasts. It's different for everyone and many different things happen. For example, a young girl, Emma, who came on a trip with us, went to the beach and cried on the Monday after'.

Roger then said: 'That's what happened to me just now'.

'Just go with it, don't worry, follow what inside wants to do. If you want we can talk about it again later.'

At home the next day, I got a call from Roger who told me more about his Dolphin Within experience: 'I was very quiet yesterday on the boat. It's very difficult to be quiet and isolated on a boat with eight people. When I arrived at my friends' place, I knew they had a room where I could go. So I went there and cried for an hour. I was very emotional, very quiet, sitting in the dark, crying, sitting on a box. The dolphin trip was an amazing experience, better than the Sydney–Hobart yacht race. I know I'll go back again. I understand now that the Dolphin Society means that there's a bit of dolphin in us all'.

Three days later I went to see Roger at his home and he told me more about his grief.

What came to me was loneliness, because my wife and I split up fifteen years ago and I've only had one relationship since then. It is hard with the knowledge I have of the dolphins, understanding that when they mate that they mate for life.

Here were these creatures, cruising in the waters ten feet away, but I couldn't see them. I wasn't worried about being injured by them. Not being able to see them, the only sensory indication I got that they were around was when I heard them breathing.

That's why on Sunday I was quiet, because I was reflecting. I wonder what it is. When I went to that friend's house on Sunday afternoon, I sat on that box in a room underneath her house. I think I probably sat for half an hour or more.

I've felt this pain before, when my wife and I separated. I was sad for a while because I had nobody to do things with, I had to start all over again. Not being able to drive is an obstacle. It isn't fun to go for a walk on the weekend, because of all the obstacles in the streets. That's part of the isolation.

I found the dolphins fascinating. I don't know anyone who doesn't find them beautiful. People get excited just to see them. I remember seeing dolphins before I lost my sight.

I had meningitis for two months when I was fourteen. They didn't know that I had lost my sight. When they put me in the ambulance to take me to Sydney again, I said to the nurse who helped me: 'When are you going to put me outside, so I can see if the sun shines?'

I was already outside in the sun, but I couldn't see it. Then they all realised that my eyesight was gone. I didn't realise until sometime later. I was so sick. I used to weigh just twenty kilos. It was a very traumatic time, to say the least, being fourteen and just starting to have an interest in girls. When I came out of the hospital, children came to my hotel to see what a blind person looks like, there was something different about me. And when I was surrounded by blind children, it made me feel worse, not better.

I don't think it's right to isolate people who have the same disability. When I lost my sight I had to learn new skills like reading braille. When I had done that I wanted to go back to high school, but they wouldn't let me do it. One of the reasons I do all the things I do now is just so that I know I can do them.

I was restricted for a long time. For example, I wanted to go swimming and there was a pool, but I wasn't able to use it without a supervisor. I've been able to swim all my life, it would have helped me. I would have been better adjusted rather than living in isolation. I wanted to be an active, involved member of the community.

When I was in the hospital, Mum slept on a banana chair in the hospital room, she just didn't want to let go. Dad and my sister were running the hotel on their own for months. When I came out of the hospital she was there for me.

She still does the same thing, she comes to my house every day if she feels she has to. Even though I'm 42, she feels that I'm unable to look after myself. I appreciate a lot of things she does for me, but other things drive me bananas.

I suppose she feels guilty. That if she'd have looked after me better I wouldn't have lost my eyesight. But I just got sick, anybody could have got the germ ... They never really knew what I had. I shouldn't be alive. The doctors said they didn't know why I was still alive.

Personal transformation

I asked: 'So what do you think are the effects of the Dolphin Within experience on you as a person, Roger?'

It has certainly changed me as a person. I've been more aware of what other people's needs are, being very aware of them. Dolphins are like women. You need to let them come to you instead of chasing them. I learnt that I needed to relax to get dolphins coming to me.

It's interesting. One thing that happened over the weekend; I certainly
don't feel the need to drink as much as I used to. Maybe another swim
with the dolphins might help me to cut it right down!

I learnt to snorkel. In the days following the weekend I went surfing in
big waves.

My resolutions after the weekend are to work three days a week instead
of five; to go onto the public speaking circuit; to drink less and to
meditate more. I used to meditate, I haven't done it for a while. I'd like to
go back.

Nine months later when I next met Roger, he was working three days a
week and he was making a successful career as a public speaker. He has since
published his biography and wants to come back to the dolphins again.

Healing cry

Roger's case illustrates one of the Dolphin Within patterns; the emotional
release that some participants experience. People burst into tears, either
during their encounters with dolphins or later on. Such emotional releases
free them from a grief or past pain that they had never really been in touch
with or found a way to express. The Dolphin Within experience brought
them right into that hidden spot, freeing them from any repression
mechanisms.

In the case of young Emma, it was the recent divorce of her parents. In the
case of Roger it was a much older pain, one that he had carried from the
time he became blind, and which worsened when his wife left him.

You may ask, why go and see dolphins, only to cry? Such crying helps
people to free themselves of the past, releasing unconscious emotions which
still operate in their lives but are hidden. Crying brings the peace inside
rather than the weight of an unknown pain. Crying is becoming real, getting
in touch with the real self: the Dolphin Within.

Roger also noticed, like many other Dolphin people, that he feels less
need for his regular addictions such as coffee and alcohol. Addictions are
certainly necessary in order to suppress and hide grief and pain. Daniel's
story illustrate that pattern in more depth.

FREE FROM ADDICTION

I saw Daniel's mother, Therese, on Monday at the psychotherapy school. She
had heard that someone had cancelled their trip at the last minute, and she
asked me if her son Daniel could come because he was in a terrible state. He
was smoking, drinking, taking drugs and depressed. She didn't know what to
do with him; he was fourteen years old.

We picked up Daniel in Chatswood on Friday on the way to Port Stephens. He was like a wild animal in a long Drizabone brown coat. He was dressed in black with big baggy clothes. His hair was long and dirty, his skin was covered with acne and he didn't make eye contact.

He joined us in the minibus and we didn't talk a lot on the way. I showed him a book of fish, and he mentioned that he used to go fishing with his father.

I let him listen to the tape of dolphin sounds I got from Gill, a biologist at Sydney University. Gill was recording dolphin sounds in the wild. A large pod of dolphins came to his boat at one point, and a woman on the deck called out 'Hello!' to the first dolphin. Gill was amazed to hear the dolphin's response, 'Hello!' through his headphones. Gill told me that he wanted to write a paper about it, but he never did because he said: 'you know it is not scientific!'

I let Daniel fill in the diving questionnaire and he said that he had had experiences with drugs and other substances. I said, 'It'll probably be okay if it's not too recent, but we have to check with the instructor. If you smoke it might be difficult to dive'.

When we arrived he wanted to smoke outside the minibus. I said 'That's the last one because you can't smoke on the boat; it's dangerous for the dive and for the other people on board. I hope you'll survive. Maybe you won't need to smoke'.

He was very slow and sleepy, waiting. I said that he had to help us, on the boat everyone helps each other. So he helped us to unload the gear from the minibus to the boat.

Some participants were missing. I was wondering how we would find Laureen and her friends, in the crowd that was there for the Easter market in Nelson Bay. I said to myself, it will just happen. I walked along the jetty and a couple saw me and shouted, 'You're Olivia!'

That was it, we were all together.

We got our diving gear from the local Pro-Dive shop, which kindly sponsored us with gear for everyone. It took an hour for Daniel to try his wetsuit. I was waiting for him. He said, 'You're like my Mum, she's always waiting for me in shops because it takes hours to try on clothes'.

'I'm not your Mum. I can be your dolphin in the water. I can show how to swim with dolphins and scuba dive, but I won't be your mother on the boat.'

Learning to be responsible

We left the port and immediately got a very good energy with Laureen, her fiance Brett and their friend Simone.

Daniel was asking, 'Where is my gear, where is my mask, my fin?'

I said, 'On the boat people are responsible for their own gear. You need to know where you left it, and also to be sure that it isn't going to fly away in the wind. I can't be responsible for you. My role is to look after the dolphins and you in the water'.

We saw some dolphins on our way to Fame Cove and I jumped in the water with them. I said to the group as I climbed back on board, 'You saw what I did, tomorrow it's your turn'.

Slowly, Daniel learnt to be responsible. He complained a lot at the beginning about the wetsuit, the fins and so on. He was very negative, but he jumped into the water in our protected cove late in the afternoon, and loved it. He even went back into the water late at night, in the dark!

Brett also jumped in the water in the dark. When he came back from his swim he said, 'I would have never done something like that in the past. I'm very scared of water in the dark. I don't know why, but I really wanted to jump in this water and swim in the dark. I felt very safe'.

That was the first breakthrough, and it was only Friday night! Another case of a person letting go of his fear.

As we left Fame Cove the next morning, we met dolphins in the middle of the bay, and everyone was ready to jump overboard. I was filming. It was good to see people excited and ready to jump, organised with their gear, their wet suits. Daniel was one of the first in the water.

On the second night we anchored at a different beach. I was concerned by the tide, and I had visions of the boat lying on the side close to rocks. William was very confident and was sure that we were not drifting.

That night Daniel and I went to the beach. We jumped off the boat to walk on the beach. I realised that he wanted to smoke. At the beginning I said no, because I don't like breathing the smoke, and also because of the dive planned for the next day. Then I let go, and I said, 'Smoke if you want'.

He then tried unsuccessfully to light his cigarette with a lighter, and I was laughing saying, 'You don't know the power of the dolphin energy, the gods are with me'.

The lighter didn't want to work, so Daniel couldn't smoke. He finally gave up and we walked back to the boat. As soon as we arrived on board, someone asked for Daniel's lighter, to make a cup of tea. Daniel grinned at me as he handed over the lighter. I was going to say: 'the lighter does not work', when I met his eyes and we both smiled.

The grin left his face a moment later. The lighter worked perfectly.

Premonition under the full moon

We spent a beautiful evening, listening to Daniel's short stories, which were very well written and full of Gothic dark and frightening adventures. We went to bed after the tea and as it was raining we slept in the cockpit under the canopy. Before going to sleep the sky cleared for a little while and we saw the moon eclipse. It was superb, with a large red auric circle around the moon.

I didn't sleep a lot because I was concerned by the tide. We were anchored in a different place than usual. I also felt connected with the large full moon. Finally I went to sleep at around three o'clock, only to be awakened again by a big jolt. The tide had gone out and the boat had fallen onto its side on the sand! Luckily, nothing was broken and as we weren't sleeping on the deck, we didn't ended up falling overboard.

We got up and Laureen and Brett joined us on the beach. The moon was full and there was a very wild spirit in the air. It was like being Robinson Crusoe, the shipwreck on the beach and the wild land behind us. I wanted to make love on the rocks!

I calculated that the tide would come back in time to let us join Jim for the dive at 7.30 a.m. We went back to bed, and I checked later on to see the water coming back to be sure that we were safe.

Diving with the dolphins

Sunday we went diving and that was another breakthrough for Brett and Daniel. Simone and Laureen had dived before and we took them to the wreck where we found plenty of fish. We also heard the dolphins around. After this fantastic experience for everyone, we went to see more dolphins. They came and made eye contact with Brett on the side of the boat, he was breathless. The baby came, splashing and rolling on its back, showing its white belly.

They followed me as I was in the water. There were two pods and one pod went to the beach as the other one followed me for a while.

As we anchored close to the beach, dolphins came close to the boat and Brett jumped into the water, he was wading and a dolphin came straight to him. I took a photo of him standing up in front of a dolphin, it was just like being at Monkey Mia.

William went snorkelling around the rocks as I was meditating on the beach. When I opened my eyes I saw William with two fins swimming just behind him. I could see him snorkelling and looking under water. I wondered if he knew that he had two dolphins next to him.

I was also laughing at myself inside. I had just spent an hour on a rope behind the boat, which is magic but still hard work, and here was William who was just snorkelling quietly and had two dolphins coming to see him. Another lesson about letting go, not grasping.

I joined him in the water later, but he went straight to the middle of the bay and didn't want to come back. I could see that he was in his dolphin experience, unable to come back.

He finally came back onto the boat and explained what had happened. 'While I was snorkelling I forgot completely about dolphins. At one point I saw a big flathead in the sand, and I heard the dolphins! They were really close. I didn't want to put my head up, I stayed face down in the water. I didn't see them, but I could hear them. I had the feeling that the dolphin was telling me "hey, that's my fish!" They were really close because the sound was amazing, going through my whole body.'

William's insights

William wrote the following in our journal:

At the beginning of the weekend, people are really excited to see dolphins. They keep asking where they are. By the end of the second day, people are less eager to see dolphins, they are more interested in becoming dolphins themselves. We're creating a space and the dolphins help, for people to open to something inside themselves. On the second day, people are more open and dolphins are all around us. It's beautiful when we see the last dolphin coming and saying goodbye as we enter the marina at the end of the trip.

The program is based on a lot of parameters to get the flow. It seems that sometimes the dolphins are less available, either that or the people are too closed. We work with an energy. I feel it's a combination of lot of things. It's not 'dolphins full stop'. It wouldn't be the same without us. It's 'dolphins plus us plus people'. It's interesting that the most successful trips have often been on the full moon, a time when people are more open.

I try to stay objective: dolphins are intelligent. Are they interested in us? Are they saying hello to us? Is it a part of the dolphin consciousness? Have they a connection at a more global level? I know that the experience is wonderful. When everybody is open to the energy, all the magical things happen.

It is about helping people to be in touch with themselves. People like Daniel who have lost touch with themselves, lost interest in life.

Cooking for the first time

Part of the Dolphin Within program is about receiving and giving, so everyone on the yacht is in charge of one meal. The last night, we all said to Daniel that it was his turn to cook. He looked at us with big eyes: 'I have never cooked. Mum cooks for me'. I said: 'It's okay; you can learn'. So, with William's help, Daniel prepared for us a fantastic pasta meal with tomato sauce and vegetables. It was really good and we all celebrated Daniel's first steps into the world of culinary art.

I have a new son

I saw Therese a week after the weekend with her son. As soon as she saw me she hugged me and said, 'I have a new son. He's stopped smoking. He's completely transformed!'

We were at the psychotherapy school. I sat down and thanked the energy, thanked my dolphin connection. I felt complete, I felt so rewarded for my efforts, just to hear that the Dolphin Within people were happy.

Therese described Daniel's transformation.

When he got home, he told me that he was giving up smoking because he wants to become a diver. He said he can't smoke. He has to look after his lungs.

He's out of his room, confident, cooking dinner. He has already cooked two really good and delicious meals. It's as if he doesn't seem to be worried about the girls or anything. He's got a life, something just for him. He's looking after his skin, he's washing. Because he wouldn't shower, I hadn't put any sheets on his bed. The other day he had a shower and I asked him what he was doing. He came out and he looked beautiful.

I told her that if inside he wants to be beautiful, so he will be beautiful outside. It was amazing that he was able to give up smoking so easily, because he made the decision. The decision had to come from him.

Therese added that following the trip, Daniel went to see a psychologist at his school and said, 'I don't want to see you any more, I'm okay now'. Apparently the school psychologist had wanted to put him on medication for his depression.

I remember from the trip an instant when I caught Daniel's eye as he was listening to what I was sharing with Laureen and Brett about John Lilly and his work on dolphins, his exploration through LSD as a way to discover spiritual worlds. I was saying that nowadays, exploring spiritual worlds is easier because they are much more accessible us; we don't need to use drugs. We can experience incredible altered states without drugs.

I wasn't talking to Daniel but I realised as I finished that he was listening too. Stolen knowledge is the best knowledge, much better than being told!

Clear about what he wants

A year later, I again asked Daniel's mother about his progress. Apparently he had left school, and had done a course to become a chef. He was doing an internship with a French chef from New Caledonia. The chef said, 'With me you aren't going to sit down in a corner and peel potatoes, you're going to really cook. Becoming a cook is working 10 hours and then discovering that the other chef is sick so you have to work even more, without sleeping. So it's hard work but when you know how to cook, you will be able to travel all around the world'.

Apparently Daniel is happy and so clean in his white chef's uniform.

Healing from depression

In May 1996, an Australian journalist wrote an article about the Dolphin Society. Daniel agreed to be interviewed. It was then more than a year after his dolphin experience. I hadn't seen Daniel face-to-face since the weekend, and I was happy to have a third party interviewing him. The journalist who went to see Daniel and his mum told me afterwards that she couldn't believe how clear he was about his life's direction. The article she wrote went as follows.

> When Daniel Style's parents divorced four years ago, he was sent spiralling into a deep depression. He started skipping school and sneaking out of his home at night. He was drinking and smoking and having problems with his friends and teachers.
>
> 'Everything was just getting me down,' recalled Daniel, a quiet 15-year-old. 'I just used to sit in my room all day and listen to music and smoke.'
>
> He was sent to the school counsellor who told Daniel's mum, Therese, that he was suicidal and needed immediate help. She thought medication was a bit drastic and decided to send him swimming with the dolphins before trying anything else.
>
> 'And it was the best thing I could have done,' smiles Therese, a beauty therapist and hands-on healer. 'Before he went he had been totally focused inwards. The dolphins seemed to teach him to look beyond himself.'
>
> She also claims Daniel grew five centimetres in the months after the swim. He found direction and decided on a career as a chef ... Now Therese is planning to send her other son, Liam, 17, on a swim too.
>
> Says Daniel, 'I think the dolphins have some sort of spiritual knowledge. I remember just watching the way they move: it's very natural, quick and graceful. I really believe they wanted to help me. I think they are loving and intelligent creatures'.

I rang Daniel for an update in September 1997:

> I finished my internship in cooking. I am now continuing study at TAFE as part of the adult education system. I am also really enjoying learning to

play guitar. I play every day. Three years after the trip, I still remember the dolphins ...

Daniel's case study showed us again how strong the process was, and how real miracles could happen. We were even more determined to understand what was happening, and keen to get an EEG machine to measure what happens in the human brain while people are in contact with dolphins. The key questions were finding the right machine, and the finance to buy it.

 ### FREE ACCESS TO STORED TRAUMA

Venus is a beautiful bush woman, who lives in the forest, plays the didgeridoo and radiates light. As soon as she was in the water with dolphins she started crying. Back on board the yacht she told me, 'The dolphins put me back in contact with a childhood memory I had completely forgotten. It's very painful. My stepfather was very cruel to me. I had a flashback to a day when he tried to kill me'.

Over the two days she experienced healing and joy from the dolphins. Her case showed us that the Dolphin Within experience could give people access to stored trauma. In Stuart's case it is shown how the stored trauma has an impact on his life, while he is not even aware of it.

Stuart went through a similar process. He arrived with Wendy who had just landed from the UK that morning for a four-week holiday. Stuart was on a six-month assignment for a large British telecommunication company. Over a cup of tea, Wendy explained that she was not comfortable in the water, so her expectation of the weekend was to overcome that fear. They were all keen about experiencing scuba diving on Sunday.

Jim, our dive instructor, organised their equipment. He gave me the following assessment: 'Olivia, I sense a lot of apprehension. I think we should let them dive in a swimming pool on Sunday morning and then in the sea.'

I trust the Dolphin Within process, so I tried to reassure Jim, who has worked with us for more than two years now, with the following: 'Jim, they are going to spend a day snorkelling in the dolphin environment, by Sunday they will be ready for the scuba dive'.

That did not change Jim's rational and professional assessment. 'I have sensed a lot of fear. I think we should dive in the swimming pool'.

I did not want to argue more. 'Jim, I will let you know by Saturday night what their decision is: if they want to dive in the pool or if they are keen to dive in the sea.'

I organised the snorkelling activities. I could look after Wendy: 'I will be your dolphin', I said. I paired Stuart with the two children: Nicole and Leander.

They left first as I was slowly putting Wendy in touch with the mask and snorkel. I told them to stay away from the current. I watched them crossing over towards the rocks to see the fish. I could see Stuart, panicking a little bit. They came back straight away. Stuart was obviously panicky, out of breath; the children were totally okay. I gave him a hand and brought him back to the yacht. I let them rest while I crossed over with Wendy.

Wendy was tense at the beginning and then relaxed as soon as she saw the fish. When we came back to the yacht, I asked Stuart if he had had a similar experience of panic before and he said no.

While we were having lunch Stuart suddenly remembered a bad experience with water. When he was kid he was canoeing and got trapped in the canoe — head in the water. 'What was even worse was that my friends were watching me and I could hear them laughing at me while I was drowning.'

Early departure, 6:30 a.m. for the dive. Everyone wanted to dive in the sea, not in the pool. Just before anchoring for the scuba diving session, we saw the dolphins. I always tell them: 'When you are diving, listen because you can sometimes hear the dolphins'. While the adults were diving, we took the children swimming with dolphins.

Depending on the dolphins' behaviours, we sometimes stop the boat and swim with them or put a rope at the back of the boat, the dolphin rope, and get pulled by the boat. The dolphins join us.

After her turn on the dolphin rope surrounded by dolphins, Nicole went to sit at the bow and literally called the dolphins while Leander and I stayed on the rope. Leander quickly caught on to my dolphin swim style. She was like a dolphin, swimming very beautifully. We swam with the dolphins along the bay, then came back with them to where Stuart and Wendy were diving. We left the diving area and as we came out of the bay, we received one of the most beautiful gift from our pod.

By that time we had both left the rope, and as I was holding Leander's hand, three large dolphins came and swam below us. The water was so clear that we could see their eyes connecting with us as they swam just below us. They were not just passing under us, they were really playing with us. They were looking at us. They seemed to like our dolphin swim. They seemed to radiate an incredible joy. Everything stopped to that instant. Leander and I were still holding hands and no rope, we were free in the dolphin world. The three dolphins left us, then suddenly reappeared below us, this time with a baby dolphin. I realised that because I was holding the hand of a young girl, the mother dolphin was bringing her baby dolphin to me.

Back on the beach, where the divers were coming out of the water, we all shared our experiences. Stuart and Wendy explained that they were feeling apprehensive about diving but when they heard the dolphins underwater, they first could not believe it. Then their fears were gone and they felt peaceful. Wendy and Stuart spent the rest of their holiday scuba diving on the Great Barrier Reef.

Leander and Nicole went back to their parents, who noticed an incredible peace and energy around them.

 ## FREE FROM SELF-DOUBT AND WEIGHT

One weekend we had aboard a school principal, Joanne, and one of her teachers, Katrina. I filmed Katrina at the beginning of the trip. She shared the following:

> I wrote this poem about a week ago as I was listening to some dolphin music and looking out to sea. It reflects my life at the time.
>
> > Oh dolphins far out to sea
> > Is life going to be good for me?
> > I hope for so much more
> > Oh how I'd love to soar
> > As high as one can get
> > And no longer shall I forget
> > To search for all there is
> > Even though I sometimes get in such a tiz
> > I want to be free
> > Oh please come and rescue me
> > From myself in times of doubt
> > When all I want to do is shout
> > But I know what I want
> > And I shall go I shan't stop
> > Till I am here alone
> > Yes dear friends I'm coming home
>
> At about the same time as I wrote the poem, I was meditating and I saw a dolphin come up to me. I was standing on a pier and I was ready to jump in the water and be with them.
>
> They said, 'Come with us, let's be free, life is wonderful. It doesn't have to be like this. You can swim with us and you can go far.'
>
> I was about to go and they said, 'No you can't come, it's not the right time, not yet.'
>
> I said, 'But I'm ready.'
>
> They kept saying, 'You're not ready, you're not ready. It's not right.'
>
> So I waited on the pier and finally they came back. I jumped in the water and I swam with them. I just swam everywhere, I thought that life

is absolutely limitless and I can do everything. That's what I'm hoping to achieve, to get through all the boundaries so I can have a limitless life.

Over the weekend, Katrina jumped in the water and swam with the dolphins. She shared the following in front of the video camera.

> I was a little anxious about getting in when it was really cold, but it feels really good. I feel invigorated [about being with the dolphins]. This has been one of my dreams for so long. I know it'll help turn my life around. I don't care what it takes. I'll do anything I have to do to achieve this. If that means jumping into the cold water, I'll do it.
>
> It's the same with my life. All I want is to be shown how to do it and I'll do it. As soon as I said that, the dolphins appeared. It was really good.

This is the poem she wrote after her dolphin experience.

> When I feel I can't go on
> And all my hopes and dreams have gone
> I see you swimming in the sea, and hear you say
> 'Come, be with me. Leave behind you all that strife
> And you and I will have a good life'
> So I do not fret, I do not worry
> I know that I will not be sorry
> For deep within your eyes I can see the reasons why
> I must journey inside me if I am going to be free
> No longer need I hide from what I feel deep inside
> To my fears I say goodbye
> No more will I cry

Katrina also discovered a love of sailing. A month later we met Joanne, who told us how Katrina had changed. 'She's now in charge of her own life, inspiring children with dolphins. She's created a dolphin room for the children, she's losing weight and she's stopped having accidents. She's joyful, and the children love her energy.'

The transformation continues

A year later, the journalist who interviewed Daniel spoke to Katrina and wrote the following:

> Schoolteacher Katrina D. was sick of being overweight. She had ballooned to 83 kg and she still couldn't stop herself from bingeing every night. She was fighting with her friends and having problems at work. She was also the innocent party in three separate car accidents all within months of each other. Then she went swimming with dolphins.
>
> 'And I came back a completely different person,' she says, smiling. 'Everything in my life felt great and things sorted themselves out.'
>
> Katrina, 25, lost more than 3 kg in the weeks after her swim and over the past ten months she has shed another 13 kg. She has dropped from size

18–20 to a much slimmer 14–16 and she says she will continue to lose weight — particularly after she goes on a second dolphin swim later this year.

'I really wanted to lose weight,' says Katrina, who has also found a boyfriend since her watery encounter with these delightful marine mammals. 'I had a bad self image. I didn't have much self-confidence but the dolphins have helped me get the weight off. There has been an amazing difference.'

She says she suddenly had the willpower to stop eating her usual fatty diet of fried takeaway foods, cake, chips and lots and lots of chocolate. She started exercising, gave up smoking and even enrolled in singing and massage classes.

'I can't explain why this happened,' says Katrina, who got a dolphin tattoo on her stomach to mark the occasion. 'It's the dolphins' eyes that get me. They're full of wisdom. It's like they're looking straight at your soul and know everything about you. I think they can tune into you and your problems. I think they're a sophisticated animal that is further up the evolutionary ladder.

'You can feel that they are around as soon as you get into the water. It's a tingling sensation in your body and since I've been on the swim, I still feel like there is a dolphin with me all the time — like a guardian angel.'

Reflecting on Katrina's story, I was happy to indirectly facilitate change and dolphin energy spread to her and the children of the school. Children do need dolphin energy with all the violence they are exposed to. In the future our work will need to reach millions of children through fiction films, CDs, cartoons and the Internet to give them hope.

 ## FREE FROM PHYSICAL PAIN

Lisa is a teenager who came with us twice. She loves dolphins, and she came alone the first time, but the second time she brought her friends Benita and Yvonne, and her mother, Ruth.

The Dolphin Within program is open to people of all ages. Lots of children and teenagers have a strong love of dolphins, which they express through posters, photos, and clothes with dolphins and dolphin jewellery. This dolphin-mania is important, and needs to be understood and respected.

Young people are looking for role models, and adults are not always the best models to follow. Dolphins represent love and fun and creativity, a kind of dream of a life they wish to have. Young people can perceive the message of the dolphins and are keen to study and learn more from them. This phenomenon is happening all over the world, bringing a global consciousness for the world to come. We see one of the roles of the Dolphin Society is therefore to give young people an opportunity to explore their relationship with dolphins.

Lisa, Benita and Yvonne had a lot of perceptions and insightful ways of describing the Dolphin Within experience on the yacht over the weekend.

'Dolphins are peaceful, beautiful, amazing, breathtaking, indescribable! It was wonderful because I forgot all my worries and I felt great,' wrote Benita.

'Since seeing the dolphins, I've been totally relaxed. I haven't been worrying about anyone else. I've just been totally immersed in my own thoughts. I laid down on the deck, and later just fell asleep. I feel really relaxed and at peace with my world,' said Yvonne. 'Dolphins are magical, wonderful, beautiful, graceful, amazing, gorgeous. I've never seen dolphins up close before. Today seeing the wild dolphins was so much more special and magical because they were not trained to come up to us, they just did! I had such an amazing adrenalin rush, but it wasn't just adrenalin, it felt like a spiritual experience.'

Over the trip I asked them about school. They were sad because there was a huge gap between schoolwork and their passion for the dolphins. I said that maybe they might be able to combine the two. A few months later, Lisa called me to let me know that she was doing an individual school project on dolphins and society. She came round to consult our books and material. William scanned some beautiful photos for her project report. She later gave me permission to reproduce some abstracts from her project report, which includes her experiences and the interviews she did with her friends that she brought to the dolphins. Months later, all of them remembered the Dolphin Within experience and gave us more details about their experience of healing, inter-species communication and spirituality. In many ways they show a lot more perception and insight than the majority of adults.

Healing arthritis

Lisa writes about dolphin encounters, starting with the first one on 26 March 1994.

> I have always had a fascination for dolphins ever since I was little and I heard through a friend about Olivia and William and their research. Even though I loved dolphins, my main purpose was to see if the dolphins could cure me, short and long term. I had been playing a lot of sport, namely netball and tennis and after I had finished playing I received agonising pains in my knees suffering from arthritis.
>
> Over the two days the dolphins came around the boat many times. I was the only one lucky enough whilst leaning over the boat to touch one! I know for sure there was a 'spiritual bond' between them and me. I

stopped getting pains and I was a lot more relaxed which felt great.

My second encounter: As time progressed my love and understanding grew larger for dolphins. I was so looking forward to it once again and I had never stopped talking about my first encounter. This time it was going to be even better as one of my closest friends Benita was joining and Yvonne and last but not least my mother, Ruth.

... Whenever we had a chance to swim we were in the water. Olivia had an encounter with five dolphins — they swam all around her. When she came out of the water she was speechless, and then she said 'It was magical'.

These two weekends were very special to me in different ways. On my first weekend I was happy to be able to see dolphins in the wild, on the second trip, observing my friends and their enjoyment of the dolphins, gave me a very special glow inside.

Sending mental messages

Lisa then interviewed Benita, and reported her encounter.

When the trip began I was feeling happy and was excited about swimming with dolphins. Our first day started grey and cold and at first there was no sight of them. I told everyone to send mind messages to them to come to us, so I sat down with Yvonne and Lisa with our eyes closed and I pictured dolphins swimming. I called out to them and practised sending mental messages. It was then that Olivia called out that dorsal fins were spotted and I couldn't believe it.

We jumped up and were calling out and whistling and calling. I was so happy. I felt I had spiritually bonded. Whenever they came close to the boat, I was overflowed with emotion. I just wanted to swim and touch them. All my problems were forgotten and for once, I felt like a young child again, happy, free, no complications, just love.

Mental image transmission

What Benita and Lisa are discovering by themselves is the way dolphins communicate by mental images. Through their sonar system, they are able to send information using sound which is reflected and transformed in their melon, what some call an 'over-developed third eye', into a holographic image. Benita and Lisa are using the same process to communicate with them. By being with dolphins, humans start exploring another way to be, finding new skills that could be developed. Dolphins are leading us through a new exploration in human potential.

Dolphin drunkenness

Lisa's interview with Benita goes on as follows:

That night was a memorable one. The adults were up on the deck singing folk songs, while Yvonne, Lisa and I were below deck laughing so hard our stomachs hurt. We had these uncontrollable laughing spasms, and we felt totally relaxed and at peace with the world.

Over the weekends we have often noticed this laughing effect in people. Benita described it very well. It might start with one person and then infect the others.

I saw William and James, his little son, laughing on the berth for hours one night. They were completely red in the face, crying and laughing. I've also been caught in this contagious laughing myself. Finally we gave it a name: we called it *Dolphin Drunkenness*. People usually need alcohol to be happy and to laugh, but with the Dolphin Within experience, we get drunk just on the spirit. That's why we have insisted on not having any alcohol, cigarettes or other drugs on board the boat, so that people can discover another way to get high.

Friends for life

Already friends, Lisa and Benita became inseparable. Both are growing into beautiful young women physically and spiritually. Lisa lost a lot of weight and has no more pain in her knees. She told me one day, 'People tell me that a normal teenager loves parties, smoking and drinking, but I can't survive with the smoke and alcohol. I don't want to be materialistic. I just like dolphins'.

Lisa is very successful at school; next year she will start university and whatever profession she will choose, she will be a person with a great heart.

The Dolphin Society fosters teenagers' growth with different values in terms of fun and joy. These dolphin souls need to have a space to meet and discover that they are not so strange, and that it is okay not to follow the dominant mould.

Facilitating miracles?

On the research side, Lisa's story of healing her physical pain surprised us, but she and her mother confirmed it a year later. At this stage we did not know how it could be possible. We started asking ourselves if we could facilitate miracles on the yacht with the help of the dolphins!

Lisa's school project concludes:

> For those people like myself and my friends, who have had the good fortune to enjoy close contact with dolphins in the wild, it can have the most uplifting and lasting effect. I believe it doesn't matter if you have a close encounter or just a split second encounter, it can change your life.

FREE TO ACCESS FULL CREATIVE POTENTIAL

Steve, a graphic designer, took part in an early program. Around the fire he expressed his passion about sculpture. He brought the only piece of sculpture he had ever done to show the group. After the program he enrolled in a sculpture class to tap into his creative potential fully. Two year later he expressed how important sculpture has become in his life:

> Sculpture has become my 'raison d'être'. It is more important than anything else. It takes up my weekends and any spare time. I have sculpted large-scale pieces of art and intend to organise an exhibition soon.

Our friend Ken, a well known composer and musician, was improvising, singing and playing guitar on the yacht. The following week, he told me on the phone: 'Since the weekend, I have been much more creative, writing new songs. I have experienced a new creative flow'. Within weeks, Ken had composed a new CD, *Dolphin Magic*.

Like Steve and Ken, many other participants have tapped into their creativity through the Dolphin Within program, often for the first time.

 ## FREE TO CHANGE HER LIFE

Ruth's story is another fascinating Dolphin Within pattern. She was part of a pod of beautiful young women who came with us one weekend. Her journal includes the following.

> I thought it was fantastic — truly magical. I felt that the dolphins were being playful as they came and swam at the front of the boat. I felt glad to see them so close. They were friendly and I was not afraid as I felt them move towards us. I feel they are peaceful creatures and you easily feel this when you see them. They are graceful, unique creatures. They also seem mysterious, as they are very different to other water creatures.
>
> One moment touched me in particular. William was singing in Latin and as soon as he started the dolphins moved towards our boat and started playing. It was like they responded.
>
> I cannot stop swaying from the boat! I feel more in touch with the water and want to contact a dolphin again. The first time was like fulfilling curiosity but the second time I felt connected with them as I watched them. I would like to see them again to watch their peacefulness.
>
> I have often had strong messages in dreams. I had a dream the second morning of the trip. I dreamt that dolphins were all around us and in fact that was the time that Olivia, William and Susan were in the water with a

pod of dolphins. I feel that I dreamt about the dolphins either because I was half awake and my body was trying to wake me up, or I feel I sensed them so started to dream about them.

Dramatic changes occur

I had a chance to talk to Ruth's mother, who is a psychologist friend, during the following weeks. I asked her if she had observed any changes in her.

> With her personality, she could be very soft and then suddenly very aggressive. She is now very easy to live with, she is lovely. She used to be very critical of me. Now there is none of that. I can see a softening, a heart opening. She had a very difficult time last year and her heart closed. She is more open now. She is also more settled. She has a new job. She said she was very touched when William started singing and the dolphins came.

A few weeks later we were pleased to receive the following letter from Ruth:

> Dear Olivia and William,
>
> Events following the Dolphin Within weekend. My life is usually full of change. I find things move along fast and develop in new ways all the time. But around the time of the weekend away I was in a transition period of my life. There were many decisions that lingered as problems and I wasn't prepared to conquer them.
>
> The weekend away helped to lift me out of my indecision, and clarify the issues that were bothering me.
>
> The dramatic changes occurred on the day after my trip away. I was employed at a seafood restaurant but was having trouble with my boss. I rang up that Monday only to find that my boss had scheduled me next to no shifts for the next week. I decided there on the phone that I should quit so as to move on to a more stable position.
>
> I am now in a full time job with a regular income (as a nurse).
>
> I've had plans to go overseas for a long time but it seemed almost impossible because I could not achieve enough money. So on that same day I decided to move back home with my parents. It was a decision that would save me a lot of money. The idea had not occurred before.
>
> In that same day I rang a guy I had been seeing for a while. As a mutual decision we decided to end the relationship. So the day after the weekend away with the dolphins was a big day where my life moved into a whole new future.

A month later Ruth's mum shared the following with William:

> My daughter is really into dolphins. She wants to save some money to go overseas and the other day she spent $30 on a CD of dolphin sounds — only dolphin sounds! It's strange; why did she buy only dolphin sounds? And she is meditating. The other day Michael [her father] came into her room, and she was meditating.

It was interesting for me, knowing that Ruth's parents* meditate, to hear their surprise about their daughter meditating. Even the more enlightened people find it difficult to understand the dolphin effect, which is another reason for us to write this book to explain it.

Awakening to her full potential

Ruth's case study illustrates another commonly observed Dolphin Within pattern: an awakening to her full potential. She could no longer accept being simply a waitress when she had a nursing background, nor to be in a relationship which was not really a relationship.

Most important, she decided to fulfil her dream. Her dream was to travel to Europe; within a few months she managed to do it, and as I am writing she is still happy discovering Europe with a plan to visit Fungi, the famous dolphin in Ireland.

The Dolphin Within experience is a catalyst for change. People become clear about their higher purpose, what they want and don't want, and they act accordingly. Their dream very soon becomes a reality. They stop procrastinating, they just do what they want to do, achieve what they want to achieve.

FREE TO ACCESS SPIRITUAL WORLDS

Adrienne's case study shows how the Dolphin Within experience can open doors to spiritual worlds. This is how she described what happened:

> It started with a whole day. On the Friday my whole day was so stressful. I just didn't think I was going to make it to meet the people that were going to take me up to Port Stephens and I was stressing, stressing, stressing. I remember seeing this girl at the bus stop, and I said to her, 'I don't know if I'm going to make it. What shall I do, shall I just stay? Shall I go and see the dolphins or not? I just feel really stressed.'
>
> And she said 'Oh no, you should go, I think you should do that more than anything'.
>
> So somehow I managed to get there.
>
> On the boat that night I had a dream about this male dolphin and I mated with him. It felt really good. It was just a short moment, it wasn't like this prolonged coming together. That morning when we went out all the dolphins were around making love and it was really amazing to see that having had the dream. I got really excited. Eventually we got in the water and I remember this one dolphin just swam underneath me and I

---

* Two years later Ruth's mother and father joined us for a Dolphin Within program, which strengthened the couple in a new phase of their life.

felt so connected to him. It was a really strong connection. I could feel the presence of that particular dolphin, it was a male dolphin. The whole time I was there on the yacht I'd see dolphins in the clouds, and I'd see dolphins in the mountains surrounding Port Stephen. I just kept seeing them everywhere.

I'd been having a lot of struggle over whether to leave my husband or not. So I got home and I drew a picture of the dolphin and I cuddled up in bed. My husband came home with his girlfriend and he said that he was seeing her again and they were going to be boyfriend and girlfriend. Part of me felt relieved. I didn't have to worry about that any more and part of me was a bit hurt. But I felt so much love in my heart and the dolphins were with me that I felt the strength to see it through. The next morning I started to be really focused on where I was going and I knew that I wasn't going to be with him any more.

I noticed something else; when I came back I started to be able to see things around people, like if they had a physical condition for some reason I could see what was inside their aura. They would be in pain and somehow the pain was enough to make me drawn to them. Just by opening a part of myself, I still don't know what it is, but I can see it around them and somehow through concentrating on that they can see it too. And because it looks like a physical thing and they can relate to it they can remove it by saying do you want to remove it. I have helped a lot of people and it has only been since I've swum with the dolphins that I've been able to see this sort of thing. I never knew I had it before and maybe I never did and they gave it to me. I'm not sure.

There's also been other experiences where I've laid down like in a meditation and I felt like this funny slight sound, a couple of times I've felt dolphins completely surround me. It's like I've become the dolphin and I've felt the nose, I didn't quite know what was happening. This was totally involuntary, it wasn't like I was making this up and imagining it. It was like it was happening to me. I felt my consciousness come to a certain point and I just felt this shape of a dolphin. It's happened about three times.

I find that every time I'm feeling a bit down I go into the ocean I feel so much better. I think the ocean itself is very therapeutic, that's one part, and I feel also that dolphins are very close. When they are together they stay like that for life, so it's about community which is something I've been interested in, and also about fun. Just enjoying life, letting go of inhibitions instead of worrying about things all the time and letting life stress and get you down. They've showed me how to have fun. Just looking at a dolphin jumping out of the water, there's so much joy.

Following the Dolphin Within experiences, many do start meditating and exploring the spiritual worlds. The Dolphin Within experience is a spiritual awakening for the ones who are ready.

FAMILY THERAPY

Following our personal dolphin experience as a 'family', we were very interested in bringing families to the dolphins to observe the dynamics and facilitate deep change and transformation for them.

A clear Dolphin Within pattern that we identify among the different family trips we have organised is best illustrated by the two following stories; of Joanne with her daughter Candice, and Yann with his daughter Gilda and his girlfriend Caroline.

Yann arrived in his old white Jaguar with Gilda and Caroline, and Joanne and Candice, their friends from Melbourne. We set sail and encountered the dolphins straight away, at Jimmy's Beach. I went into the water then, paddling on the surf ski.

When I was surrounded by the dolphins, I asked them to go to the boat. They immediately split into two pods; one pod swam towards the beach, while the other went straight to the boat.

This weekend was really about letting the dolphins come to us. As we were anchored on the 'Dolphin Pacific Highway' (as we call the route they often seem to follow across the bay), they kept passing in front of the boat. The sea was flat and calm. The sun was shining. It was magic from the beginning.

Then I went on the surf ski with the children, the dolphins were surrounding us. I could see how much the children' energy resonated with them. I could see that Gilda was living on their frequencies.

We all returned to the boat and as we moved off I joined Caroline at the bow and asked her about her dream. She said that the previous year she had lost her baby and she felt that all her creativity had disappeared with it. She said that she would like to reconnect with it again over the weekend.

We went walking on Jimmy's Beach. Yann and Caroline went into the dunes, the children stayed with William.

I walked with Joanne. I could sense that she was separated from her partner but I didn't say anything. We started talking about Candice. I mentioned how beautiful she was, and also how she was always asking me for permission to do things, while I kept saying, 'Be what you want, you can do anything you like'.

Joanne then said, 'I don't know if I told you, but I left my husband at Christmas. Everyone expects me to be sad, but I'm not'.

I then shared with her my way of separating from partners, the learning from them and the celebration. I quoted my Mum's realisation, 'My daughter has fantastic love stories and also fantastic "divorces", because she somehow manages to stay friends with her ex-partners'.

Joanne was very happy to be able to share her feelings with someone, and to get confirmation that it was okay to be happy even when going through a divorce. She talked about her Mum, who was upset. We really connected at a deep level that morning by walking on the beach and I could see how naturally my therapy or self-development program happened; much more natural than in an enclosed room!

I shared my story and my truth. 'It's important to follow your truth and not to sacrifice yourself. So many women want to be good mothers, but end up sacrificing themselves to their children. Instead of being happy they end up resentful. Children are like dolphins, they can pick up vibes, they know exactly what's going on in the family, whether there's love or not. What they need is adults who are able to follow their vision, adults who can tap into their own full potential and who are not scared. Children have so few examples or role models of parents who love, really love unconditionally like the dolphins, love without trade!'

At night, while the children slept, Joanne mentioned how Candice loved me. She said. 'You'd be such a good mother'.

I said, 'I know, but I don't want to be a mother because I look after the children who have already grown up. They're all my children'.

'Yes, but it's different when they're your own children,' she said.

I said, 'For me, the key is to love them as they are, to trust that they will be okay, and to PLAY with them!'

Family playfulness

Yann mentioned that night that he had a strong fear of sharks. When he was a kid there was a big siren on the beach, the shark alarm. And he can still hear the voice, 'Keep out of the water'. Like many Australians, he still has the programming operating today, when the danger is gone.

I explained how there are some sharks that are totally safe and how as divers we often dive with sharks. When Yann was snorkelling on Sunday morning, he called Caroline to come and see a shark: a wobbegong.

As they both shared their shark experience, I suggested to Joanne that she try the surf ski. As I watched her rowing away from the yacht, I could see the dolphins joining her for a ride. She returned to the yacht ecstatic. Following that encounter, Joanne started playing with the children and got really high, 'Dolphin Drunkenness', as we call it.

I was filming the whole scene from the yacht, feeling content, because everything was again just so perfect: people who needed to work on their fear of sharks were meeting a shark; people who needed to get the joy of the dolphins were meeting the dolphins.

Whenever I intuitively feel that an individual is to receive the Dolphin Within gift, I try to capture the moment on video. Often at that point the sunlight plays with the camera and a triangle of light appears on the screen while the dolphin energy is working on the people.

I'm always amazed by the richness of the transformation process for everyone, including William and myself. While we were at Jimmy's Beach, William wrote *I LOVE YOU* in big, flourishing letters in the sand, which is a lot for an anglo-saxon lover! He is opening more and more to his love and expressing it more freely, just as he is opening more and more to the energy and the joy.

I continually realise how important it is to let the energy of the bay work on the people. Apart from facilitating the playshop,* caring for people sailing, floating, swimming, snorkelling, scuba diving, sharing people's pains and dreams, filming, taking photos, cooking and playing with the dolphins, my essential role is to tune in and resonate and trust the energy of love of the dolphins. At night I always ask the dolphin energy to heal and help the people on the boat.

I realised that the Dolphin Within experience is not just about seeing a dolphin, but staying in their environment, the energy of the bay is just extraordinary because one hundred dolphins live there permanently. Even when we don't see them, we feel them, their sounds travel in the water, we are in their world, and we are in their magic.

Over the weekend I observed these two beings, a mother and a daughter, getting closer to each other, accepting each other's journeys, cuddling and caring for each other, and more importantly playing with each other. The strong mother becoming the playmate. We had a big hug and a promise to keep in touch. I told her she was part of the family now. Joanne said, 'It's a link for life'.

I also observed two people who were supposed to be lovers, being quite distant from each other. Caroline's issue was around her love for Yann. They had been together for two years and it was obvious that his work and his daughter came before her. She was often by herself on the boat while Yann was playing with his daughter.

* Playshop is a term used by our great friend Dr Horace Dobbs, who says: 'I have stopped working, so I run playshops'.

Strengthening the bonds between parents and children

We received a letter from Candice and Joanne.

> Candice seems to be back to her normal self again, at last. She certainly took her time! I was starting to get a little impatient with her behaviour, so it's really nice to be able to relax and enjoy each other's company again. She actually did this painting [a dolphin painting for me] as soon as we got back home. Things seem to come in cycles and we both seen to be heading for an 'up' phase at the same time, so that's kind of nice.
>
> Please both keep up your good work. I know that people are benefiting from what you both do. Onwards and upwards with much love, Joanne and Candice.

A month later we had a dolphin dinner with Yann, Caroline and Gilda. We watched the film of the weekend, and Yann said that since then he had spent a lot of time snorkelling with Gilda. Like Joanne and Candice the connection between the parents and their children is strengthened through play.

Separation with Love

After Gilda went to sleep that night, Yann told us that Caroline and he were going to separate. 'We realise that we each have to follow a different path'.

We told them that they weren't the first couple to separate following a Dolphin Within program; we shared with them the story of Esther.

Esther arrived on our little yacht with her husband, an accountant, her teenage son and a huge family suitcase. Over the weekend, no one from the family could find any clothes in this suitcase. I saw it as a metaphor of their materialistic world. I wondered what they would learn from the program.

I observed them getting closer, particularly on the Saturday night when they all went in the dinghy, the sunset working on them. William filmed the scene as we knew it was a special time for the family to receive some healing.

As they left the yacht on Sunday night, Esther told me, 'Olivia, I've been trying to leave my husband for a year now with no success. He has never wanted to let go, and over the weekend, he told me that he now understands that we are different and that maybe I'm right and we should part'.

Shortly after, they separated and divorced in the same year. There was no drama and they remained friends.

Listening to Esther's story, Yann and Caroline agreed that they had a similar pattern; our dinner finished with joy in spite of the situation. I felt that with the dolphins and us sharing stories, we supported Yann and Caroline to follow their path. When I talked to Caroline a year later, she told me how much happier she was now, doing her own thing.

The Dolphin Within experience seems to bring clarity about what people have to do. The playshop acts as a catalyst, prompting separation for the couples who aren't supposed to be together and bonding the ones who have a higher connection. Many couples have strengthened their relationship through the Dolphin Within experience, providing each other a space of unconditional love, like William and myself, and feeling this Dolphin Drunkenness each time they hug each other.

DOLPHINS TRAINING HUMANS

Since the 1960s, people have tried to train dolphins to become puppets. As I prepared the table below, summarising the ten patterns we have observed, I realised what kind of training dolphins have given to us.

Dolphins 'train' humans to become fearless, griefless, free of addiction, free of repressed memories, free from pain, self-confident, creative, purposeful, unconditional lovers and connected with spiritual worlds!

These are the qualities we and our people aboard *Sirius* have developed by living with dolphins. Dolphins are a role model for humans, they offer us a vision of what we could become in terms of brain functioning, relationships, social and planetary transformation.

Typical Dolphin Within Patterns		
Pattern 1:	Prue	Freedom from phobia around water. Stress free and fast-tracking learning of skills.
Pattern 2:	Roger	Freedom from grief through a liberating emotional release.
Pattern 3:	Daniel	Freedom from addictions, depression
Pattern 4:	Venus & Stuart	Freedom from stored traumas or suppressed memories.
Pattern 5:	Katrina	Freedom from self-doubt.
Pattern 6:	Lisa	Freedom from physical pain.
Pattern 7:	Steve	Freedom to access creative potential.
Pattern 8:	Ruth	Freedom to change destiny for a purposeful life.
Pattern 9:	Adrienne	Free access to spiritual worlds.
Pattern 10:	Joanne & Candice	Freedom to experience unconditional love.

That is the training I had the privilege to follow and to offer to hundred of others. In the process William and his children, like myself, have been transformed by the dolphins, as the following chapter relates.

7

GOING 'BACKWARDS'

Though the search for extra-terrestrial intelligence may take a very long time, we could not do better than to start with a program of rehumanization by making friends with the whales and the dolphins.

*Carl Sagan**

FREE TO CHANGE DESTINY

As I swam with the dolphins more and more, I started to practise what I called my dolphin swim, which is a kind of butterfly stroke with a long body undulation. One weekend, William called me as he was in the water, 'Olivia, watch me!'

He dived deep into the blue water of the bay, and came up fast, throwing his body into the air, then he fell back to the surface on his side, like a whale breaching! I looked at him, and my inner voice said, 'This guy isn't going back to an office'.

When we started the Dolphin Society and our management consulting company, William was (from Monday to Friday at least) a very traditional and respectable transport-planning consultant, advising the government on transport issues.

This man who was 'whale breaching' before my eyes was supposed to go back on Monday to an office, with a tie and a smart business suit, and write a report? This man was going to resign from his job soon, I had no doubt about that!

Resigning was not a simple decision for William. He had been working for his company for 23 years! As a young student, he was recruited and sponsored by the company to study, and he become an exemplary consultant, working in various places in the United Kingdom and the Middle East before moving to Australia to open an office in Perth. After three years there, he moved to Melbourne and then Brisbane, before settling in Sydney.

---

* Carl Sagan, *The Cosmic Connection,* Doubleday, USA, 1973.

Leaving his company was as significant as leaving his family. He was one of the technical directors, and his boss was a close friend. Since his divorce two years before we met, and the separation from his children, the company was the only stable cocoon William had left to him. That year, he had lost his mother (his father had died fifteen years before). The company was really his only tie with the past.

Leaving the company meant saying goodbye to the security of a large salary, a company car and a predictable life.

Staying in the company meant going back to another life every Monday, feeling 20 years older. Each time I visited William in his office I couldn't help thinking how old he looked compared with when he was on the boat.

THE LAST TEMPTATION

It took nearly a year for William to leave the company. He made the decision at Easter 1994, told his boss late in 1994 and gave three months' notice, and walk out the office in March 1995. When he resigned, his boss Peter offered him a new position within the company with a 50% increase in salary (from $100 000 to $150 000) — a good executive salary and the 'last temptation'. William looked at him, holding the table, saying, 'No, I'd prefer to leave for the dolphin project'.

William demonstrated an incredible commitment to the dolphins by resisting the temptation to stay in this comfortable life. It was also a deep commitment to himself in terms of following his dream.

His plan was not only to resign but to buy a boat for the dolphin research. With his inheritance from his mother and his long service pay, he bought a yacht and a minibus (which I dubbed 'The Bubble') so we could conduct the Dolphin Within research.

Turning forty, turning your back on a lifetime's security and putting all the money you have into a yacht and a minibus to do some research on dolphin therapy was pretty scary stuff, but that's what William did!

I was amazed. I could observe him going through an incredible change process, the Dolphin Within process, a similar training to that which I had been through a year before. I could see him following an inner knowingness that was beyond any rational thinking. William was starting to become a role model and his story was as important as my own in order to understand the power of the Dolphin Within.

I could understand and trust the process William was going through, but not everyone could. My mum, in particular, freaked out. She was just coming to terms with the fact that, as she said on the phone, 'With your PhD and MBA, your only desire is to swim with dolphins instead of making money!'

She had relaxed a bit after meeting William — stability, calmness and wisdom incarnate. When we told her that he had resigned and bought a boat for the dolphin project, she virtually gave up on us (but only for a while!)

MONEY AS A MEANS, NOT AN END

What surprised people was that we did not set out to make money. Our main goal in life was not to be rich. We needed a lot of money in order to achieve what we wanted to achieve, but it was a byproduct of our vision, a means, and not an end. That was exactly the message we wanted to share with the business community; as soon as you start to have a higher purpose in life, a vision which goes beyond the bottom line, the money comes anyway. It looked great in theory, but we came very quickly to experience it in practice!

In May 1995, as we were driving to Port Stephens for another Dolphin Within weekend, William told me: 'By the way, I have no more money'.

I must admit that I got quite a shock because as a planning consultant I assumed that he was planning his finances and would know how to manage his cash flow. But William had been spending money the way he was accustomed to, despite having no income. That day he went to the cash machine and discovered he had no more money.

After a beautiful weekend with the dolphins, I went into a very deep meditation state, on the Monday in the dolphin room in our unit in Sydney. For the first time, I was asking for help for us. I always ask for help for the participants of the Dolphin Within program once they open and share their pain. For the first time I was asking for help for both of us and the kids.

In less than a week, a brief came through the fax machine from the Quality Society of Australasia for a special project. It was the first proposal I received from them, after being in their database for two years. Out of the 24 consulting companies invited, we won the job ($20 000) and we got our first consulting project together, working in the building and construction industry, which brought our skills together: me as a quality management consultant and William with his civil engineering background. Dolphinicity was at work!

In this way, the consulting fees allowed the Dolphin Within research to progress, while the business world was benefiting from the results of the research. We were creating a 'virtuous circle' between ODB Consulting and the Dolphin Society.

THE CORPORATE DOLPHINS

Following our 'financial crisis', we realised that we could survive anything. I also felt it was important to assume fully our responsibility towards William's children. As role models, we showed the children that it was possible to follow our dreams and do things that nobody dared to do, while still supporting them financially. As a couple, it was okay to buy a yacht to study dolphin therapy, provided we were also able to support the children in Melbourne, and bring them for holidays with the dolphins too.

It was a good test to face the fear of lacking money, which is a force that drives many people. Most organisations today are run either by fear or by greed. It was important for us to become Corporate Dolphins, rather than just spouting nice words. Since that time, the company has been growing steadily and we have always been able to balance work and research. About twice a year, William gets involved in transport planning projects. He is able to combine his rational and economic approach with his care for the environment by being a Corporate Dolphin. Free from the constraints of pushing a company line, he is now able to advise the government on transport planning with a more holistic view, for the sake of protecting the environment for future generations. Instead of cutting through a mountain to build a huge highway, destroying trees and habitats, the Corporate Dolphin strategy finds creative solutions, aimed at long-term sustainability.

Becoming his own boss and part-owning the company gave William the same freedom I have. He can put the company at risk for the sake of the client's change process, to say and do what is right for the Corporate Dolphin rather than trying to please the client to ensure that the money is coming in.

UNCONDITIONAL LOVE

My relationship with William grew out of the dolphin adventure. William was certainly not as romantic as my French lover, he virtually never brought me flowers at home, but he has always been with me, such as when I had my motorbike accident. He is the man who bought a yacht for both of us to go and live with the dolphins. I respected him and honoured him. He is the man who accepted my craziness about dolphins, and let me explore fully my connection.

William and I have become an incredible combination. I have the dolphin's energy, which is a very fast vibration, while William is more like a whale, peaceful and calm. He incarnates the wisdom of the planet. I like to wake up early in the morning to watch the sun rising and meditate and swim. William loves spending the night on the computer, surfing the net, updating our

Internet page and creating new web pages for our clients and then has difficulties waking up early.

William loves details, I love looking at the big picture. William is quiet and calm. I talk a lot and express my feelings and love sharing.

William isn't jealous. I had always had men who were jealous and frightened of losing me. They always ended up losing me. A self-fulfilling prophecy. William doesn't have this fear. He always says, 'Being your partner isn't my *sole* purpose in life'.

When we had our underwater marriage on Rapa Nui we agreed to give each other unconditional love, each allowing the other to be, no conditions or rules. We wanted a space to be, to accept whatever we each have to go through as we grow. This total acceptance of the person is another dolphin principle.

So I brought chaos into William's life, and I became the catalyst of change for his growth. I also gave him a home by the sea. He gave me a boat to stay with the dolphins. We learnt a lot from each other, and we are still learning.

We are testing the strength of our relationship by living, working and researching together. We are together 24 hours a day, seven days a week. In term of unconditional love training you cannot do more. I always found it easier to love someone when we spent the day away from each other, and met at night in bed.

Our love means sharing everything, from meditation, swimming, showers, breakfast, ten hours of work, lunch and dinner and more hours on the computer, and many weekends on the yacht and in the water with the dolphins. In this situation love is no longer an attraction, a fall, it becomes an act of will, a choice and an incredible self-transformation process for the two partners. We always say that we have lived together for three years, but we have the feeling that it's more than twenty years, because we know each other as no other souls have known us. We also know that we will never stop learning.

Whatever happens when we are in conflict, we always say that we do not want to lose what we are building together. So we stay together not because we need each other but for our common vision, our shared dream and the fact that when we are together we can really create magic for others. We realise how much the dolphin research has been our training ground to be able to incarnate a peace and hold an energy for the big responsibilities to be given to us in terms of leading individuals, teams and organisations through change.

We needed this training to be at peace inside and with each other, before being able to be responsible for making a difference on a global scale.

We know that at one point we will separate, in the sense that we will be called to work and support people at different points on the globe. We also know that following our dolphin training we will be able to communicate with each other regardless of the distance.

SIRIUS BUT NOT SERIOUS

When we started the Dolphin Within project, our vision was to have our own boat. We dreamt about the boat for a year. Each Dolphin Within program, we sang our favourite song:

> The water is wide, I can't cross over,
> And neither have I wings to fly,
> Build me a boat that can carry two,
> And both shall row, my love and I.

And then one day the dream became a reality. When *she* arrived from California on a big cargo ship, William couldn't believe that he had a yacht. We went to see her and I filmed him saying, like a kid, 'It's my boat, it's my boat!' It was so beautiful to see this man, just turning forty, in touch with his inner child and being so happy, announcing that he is going 'backwards'. William indeed looks younger now than he did five years ago!

William called the yacht *Sirius* for a lot of reasons. Sirius, the brightest star in the sky, is mythologically associated with dolphins. There are some fascinating ancient legends that say that dolphin-like beings came from there to sow the seeds of civilisation on Earth. Sirius was also the name of the flagship of the First Fleet; the ship's name was changed en route to Australia. The fleet was following the star Sirius, which is also represented on the Australian flag.

When William put the name on the boat, he put two stars in place of the dots on the 'i's in *Sirius*. These two stars represent us, our love and our connections. It also represents the fact that Sirius is actually a binary star, Sirius A and Sirius B, that is, two stars revolving around each other.

Each time we go aboard *Sirius*, we think of William's dear mother whose death allowed the dream to come true. William always says that she would have been so happy to have met me and to know what we are doing for other people with the money from her house in England. *Sirius* is our temple. To William she represents both his mother and his father, who was a very keen sailor, a man with a passion for the sea that he never fully shared with his children.

PASSAGE OF INITIATION

The next step was to bring *Sirius* to the dolphins of Port Stephens. We organised with our friend Bill, an experienced yachtsman, to take *Sirius* from Sydney to Port Stephens together. We sailed from Sydney to Brooklyn, on the Hawkesbury River, during the day, then we left Pittwater late at night to sail to Port Stephens. It was a beautiful, moonless night when we started.

As we sailed north, a southerly wind picked up and the sea heaved around us. I slept a lot at the beginning of the trip. Then William got seasick, and I got sick through seeing him. In the middle of the night, William went to sleep.

At one point, as the wind increased even more and a strong gust got our sail, Bill gave me the wheel while he tried to reef the sail. The wind and the sea were so strong that the sail was swinging wildly, Bill was hanging on for dear life. I couldn't reach the mainsail to help him. The only thing I could do was to ask for help, to be sure that Bill would not be taken overboard by the wind.

As I did so, suddenly about twenty common dolphins appeared around the boat. William surfaced from the cabin, and the wind dropped enough for him to help Bill reef the sail. The dolphins leapt in the water at our bow, flashing though the water like beings of light, their bodies lit by the phosphorescence in the moonless night. They helped us forget our fears and get on with the job!

They came three more times in the night. Common dolphins are smaller and faster than bottlenoses. It was just amazing to see them jumping and playing around the boat.

Sirius got her dolphin initiation. William got his sailing initiation. I got my out-of-body initiation. Through the seasickness I suddenly found out how I could get out of my body (seasickness is close to death!). As soon I realised this, I was out, and I could see the boat from the top of the mast, sailing. It was a quick flash, because as soon I realised what was happening I came back into my body.

When we arrived in Port Stephens the dolphins there came to welcome us. The short, violent voyage was a rite of passage. We had to go through the pain and suffering together, William, *Sirius* and I, to mark our common commitment and care.

FAMILY TEAM BUILDING

A month later, William's children joined us for their Easter holiday and to celebrate *Sirius*. It was planned as a simple holiday with William and his children (Rory, Clare and James), but it turned out to be even more transformational than usual for everyone.

It's easy to love each other from Sydney to Melbourne on the phone, or when we occasionally see each other for Christmas. The weekend was also a test. Fifteen months earlier, in January 1994, on our first Dolphin trip together, the message from the dolphins was that we were a family. Now it was time to test the validity of the message and to see if we were a family. Were we going to survive as a team through the four days, through the wind, cold, lack of comfort, cooking, washing and so on?

At the beginning, I organised and coordinated everyone's job on the boat. I felt it was important to set up the teamwork concept from the beginning so that everyone would be in charge of their own gear and enjoy helping each other. I didn't want to play the role of mother on board.

James was very frightened by the waves because, as he said to me, 'I was stuck in a wave one day. I was by myself and then I swam back to the beach'. At night he was sick, with high fevers. He was sad, missing his Mum. My inner voice told me, 'Trust the process, let him do it at his own pace'.

After that, I stopped pushing and let him be what he wanted to be. If he wanted to be sick, he could be sick.

At night, while I was cuddling William, on the deck in our double sleeping bag (our Easter gift), William expressed his sadness. He felt that the children were so different from him. They didn't have his values and way of living. He was also worried for James. I then said, 'You're sharing your life, you went snorkelling with them, it's a beginning'.

In the night James cried and asked for his Dad. He had pain in his ear. William said later, as we cuddled under the moon and two eagles made love in the air, how sad he was for James, who lacked so much self-confidence. 'He's sick and he doesn't want to snorkel. There's always been a problem between him and Rory. His elder brother has been a little bit jealous ever since he was born. He has always fought with his brother and James has always been the one to suffer.'

I said, 'Trust the process. We were able to shift Daniel, we'll be able to heal James. We have the process with the dolphins, to transform and unblock. James needs love, Rory and Clare need to realise that they can't go on like that, telling him that he's stupid all the time. We can do something about it. Love's the key. We have the Dolphin energy with us. He'll be a good case study for our research!'

The following day, while I was thinking: 'this weekend I will rest and the dolphins will come to us; we can test music and meditation, there is no hurry to see dolphins', one dolphin came straight to the boat and stayed under my hand for a long time. It was like a gift and a welcoming. Welcome back to our world. We had just come back after two days in Sydney where I had to work.

Rory, who had been with us for his birthday six months before, was quite confident in the water. He went snorkelling with Clare and William. As I watched them from the beach, I could see Clare and William reconnecting with each other though the water. While they were snorkelling together, I could see the dolphin energy working on them. The link was cleared and reconnected on a healthy and watery level. I realised even more how much my work is about healing in the water. I could clearly see the energy working on both of them as they were swimming next to each other, holding hands in the water and sharing the discovery of fish life and the underwater garden.

I don't know how research can show this 'scientifically', but something special happens if you hold hands while swimming. Maybe one day we'll be able to have our brain tested while we are doing it! It's as if a 'current of love' passes through the touch, and flows between the two people. I have experienced that in diving, when I looked after students and also when I was learning to dive with my instructor.

That morning, James was feeling better and we went together swimming. I was his dolphin, he was on my back, holding me tight. I could feel that he was very apprehensive. He did not want to join the others who were snorkelling. We stayed together by the beach in shallow waters. I asked him if he had a bad experience with the ocean and he told me that once he was nearly drowned by a big wave. 'Interesting', I thought, 'a similar experience to that of his father'. James is indeed a replica of William as a child. I could feel that he was not ready to break through, so I helped him to go back to the yacht, to get warm and relaxed.

Clare, William and Rory saw a lot of fish and seaweed. Clare wrote in the journal: 'I used to be frightened of seaweed, but I touched it and it's soft'.

As I observed Clare, I could see that she was getting more and more comfortable in the water. However, she was still very shy about her body. She was wearing the wetsuit plus a T-shirt on top, concerned by her weight on that first and second day.

On the first night, we went for a short trip in the dinghy and I asked Rory and Clare about their dreams in life. I also reminded them that last time they came to Sydney, I had asked them the same question and Clare had said, as we were visiting sailing boats in Newport, 'I wish Dad and Olivia would buy a boat so we could come on holidays with them'.

As her wish had come true, it was time to have another one.

Rory said, 'I want to be in a band'.

'But you're part of one already,' said Clare.

'Yes, but I want to be part of a successful one,' he replied.

People often have special dreams on the boat, so I often ask them about their dreams each morning. James had a dream about dolphins the night before the trip. 'I saw a dolphin coming to me in the water. Dolphins were coming to help!'

On the second day, the boat was already full of love and cuddles; the healing was in place. The dolphins came to Rory while he was playing the keyboard. I filmed an incredible dolphin encounter; they came and danced on their backs to the music, with their flippers in the air as if they were applauding him.

They also came to the back of the boat to say hello to William, who was calling them. He said, 'I'm going in for once; it's my turn!'

Another 'dolphin effect' to observe; even the captain can't resist! I took the wheel and he quickly jumped in behind, holding the rope. He had a great time, with the pod coming around the boat while Rory played his music.

When he came back on board, William explained: 'At one point I couldn't breathe, I was starting to swallow water. The boat was going really fast and I started to panic. At that moment, a lone dolphin came swimming under me, very close. I wanted to take a picture but the water current was too strong. I then felt safe and happy, with no fear'.

That night I organised a fire with the children and William started playing guitar and singing. Rory came and kissed me on the chin. I disappeared by the sea to cry. I realised that was my Dolphin Within effect.

William took the children back to the boat in the dinghy, then came back to get me. I was meditating by the fire by that time. I was in a very deep stage and I said what I was feeling: 'I believe that the world to come is about this love we experience when we are with the dolphins. It might take time, but it will come. Love is the key for healing'.

The energy was very strong as I spoke. We both laughed and cuddled, the night was beautiful. We went back to the boat and rested in each other's arms, under the stars.

ANOTHER FAMILY FEELS THE EFFECT

The next day, we welcomed Peter and his family aboard. Peter was William's ex-boss. He and his Japanese wife, Aikiko, have three children: John, Naomi and baby James.

Dolphins at play off Monkey Mia (above) and Port Stephens (below)

My father (centre) with my brother and mother (front).

Meditating on Rapa Nui, 1988.

My brother Henry with Jacques Cousteau

My PAST...

of Darkness!

My optimistic
out look of
My FUTURE

Through art, Diane
expresses her feelings
about her life before
and after the Dolphin
Within experience.
See page 104

Bluey the groper beneath the waves at Clovelly (Photo: James Alcock)

New South Wales Premier, Bob Carr, launching the campaign against littering and ocean pollution. Bluey was the star of the campaign.

Olivia with Burnum Burnum – 1996.

Campaign painting by Howie Cooke.

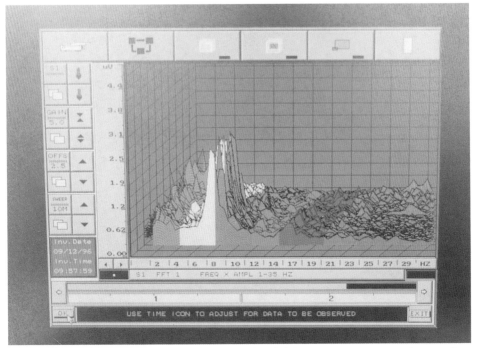

An electroencephalograph (EEG) recording of a dolphin encounter. Note the greatly increased theta (yellow) and alpha (brown) readings at the forward half of the graph as compared with the pre-encounter reading to the rear.

Olivia and a companion experience an encounter with dolphins, Port Stephens, April 1997.

Sirius moored at Fame Cove

Peter Shenstone, the Dolphin Legendarian

Dolphins at Monkey Mia

Dolphin Within smiles.

The wind started to blow strongly as we left the marina. I asked the dolphins for help. I asked for an accelerated Dolphin Within program for them, as they were only with us for a few hours.

They certainly got a crash course! We saw the first dolphin just as we left the port. This of course relaxed the atmosphere, and bonded the team. We set the sails. Peter was at the wheel, in the strong wind. We anchored off Jimmy's Beach, and the wind was so strong that it was difficult to row ashore in the dinghy. They had to face the waves, the wind. John went snorkelling with Rory and me, while Clare and Naomi went for a walk and William followed them with Peter and James. Aikiko rested on the beach with her baby, recovering from her seasickness.

We organised two dinghy trips back to the boat. Peter rowed, and told me it reminded him of the Isle of Wight, where he grew up. I was behind the dinghy in the water, kicking with my fins to help him to go against the wind. Peter saw two dolphins that came close to the dinghy, to give us more energy to face the wind.

As we sailed away again, I was in a dolphin mood. When everything seems chaotic, I feel good, I trust the process. I felt that I was going to swim with dolphins soon. I kept my wetsuit on. As we crossed the bay the dolphins came to the boat, scores of them, I was on the rope behind the boat and I could hear them. They were escorting us. One of them came swimming underneath me.

Everyone on the boat was so excited. They couldn't believe their eyes!

I came back on board and filmed Peter, who said, 'When the dolphins came, I felt excited, free and happy'. His son John said the same, 'Free and happy'.

Aikiko said that she felt sick as soon as we left the port. 'I always feel seasick when I'm on a boat, but as soon as I saw the dolphins, it went away.'

Everyone was feeling incredibly happy. Rory made a fantastic couscous for lunch. They had never heard about couscous and enjoyed it a lot.

Again I observed with pleasure the teamwork within our pod. Rory, Clare and James looked after our guests as I had asked, and they did a fantastic job.

We all went back to The Anchorage; the children had a great time in the swimming pool, playing with a ball.

It is at that point that I observed James' breakthrough. He started to snorkel by himself in the swimming pool. He did not asked for any help. He just did it quietly in his own time. Another dolphin effect to record.

He started with his mask, then the snorkel, then the fins. By the end of the afternoon he didn't want to get out of the swimming pool. I always believe that there's no need to teach people snorkelling. If we put them in a safe learning space with dolphins interacting, they discover by themselves. It is as if they know inside, it is just a question of letting the knowingness emerge from within. The dolphins help a lot by giving them a role model.

We left Peter's family at The Anchorage and we went to our little cove to prepare a fire on the beach and cook potatoes. We ate, sang and played music.

WE STOP EATING FISH

The next day, we all got up early to go and meet the dolphins. They were there and I swam with them. To my surprise, Clare jumped into the water with me. I was pleased to see her being so brave. We had a great time even though the dolphins didn't seem to want to play much. What happened was very peculiar. A dolphin came towards us twice, throwing a fish into the air. I later realised that he was telling us that they were feeding.

We went to Jimmy's Beach where I then went for a swim. I went right out to the end of the point, and swam a lot like a dolphin. I saw plenty of fish, and a big ray. I felt very free.

We then went back to the dolphins. Swimming without a wetsuit was so exhilarating. I could stay underwater longer. I felt that I was a dolphin, and that I didn't need to breathe. Another dolphin effect.

We moved on, snorkelling and then came upon something very disturbing — dead fish, stingrays, sharks and baby sharks, almost certainly the result of a fishing trawler dumping its unwanted catch in the bay. When we returned to the marina we had another shock. A game fishing competition was happening that day outside the bay. One of the sharks was huge. I'll always remember his eye, which seemed to look at us as he was hauled out of the boat. We were very sad, especially after we had spent so much time in the water with the fish.

I made a promise to myself never to eat fish again, because they were all my friends. When I shared my feelings with William and the children, they all said the same. We all decided to stop eating fish.

THE FATHER WITHIN

What was clear from the weekend was that William had connected with his children. He had said at the beginning that they didn't share his values. By the end of the trip, he was very close to them. When they left, he missed them more than usual. They spent the first night at home on the phone, and they were already talking about the next trip to Sydney. It was a breakthrough for William. Through the adventure, he discovered that he could look after his children, cook with them and play with them. He hugged them a lot and said 'I love you, je t'aime'.

It was beautiful to see the father flourishing in him. It was as if he was in touch with it for the first time. The real father, not the one who follows society's norms.

During the trip, little James learnt some French words from me, copying my 'bonjour, au revoir, bonjour, au revoir'. He also started to say to his Dad: 'I je t'aime you'. ·

OUR BEST CREW

A year later, we had another trip with the children, our anniversary! This time everything was so simple. Rory, Clare and James are our best team, they cooked and organised the beds on the yacht for us, while we had a dinner with Peter, William's ex-boss, who happened to be at The Anchorage just like the year before.

Our family pod is happy, we don't even need to talk, they are just happy to be with us. They have learnt to sail, to snorkel and to do the dolphin swim. Even James was feeding the fish with joy, resplendent in his new wetsuit.

Close to the end of our trip, we sailed on *Sirius* to Fly Point for a last snorkel. As we were snorkelling, the dolphins joined us. I was wearing my dolphin fin, and one particular dolphin came to us and made eye contact underwater with James and Clare. Clare said excitedly, 'He came and talked to me!'

It was amazing that it just happened, like a gift given to all of us. I asked my usual question of Clare about her dream, and this time she said that she wants to do marine biology to work with the dolphins like we do.

Rory's dream to have a band was becoming a reality. He had a new love, Emma. She was supposed to come with him, but at the last minute her mother forbade it because she failed her maths test. She was 14 and lost her father three years earlier. I was thinking to myself that she was a perfect Dolphin Within candidate.

When asked about his dream, James said that he wanted to become a great basketball player.

When they were leaving, I was sad; I was already missing them. They were going back to Sydney with William while I stayed to wait for a group that was coming for a Dolphin Within program. James gave me a long cuddle. He just came into my arms, said 'I love you' and stayed on my heart for a long time. Like a dolphin, he had perceived my sadness and was giving me love. It was just what I needed.

It was beautiful to see the three children growing and sharing more and more our life and our passion; to see how they loved and supported each other as they travelled on the bus to and from Melbourne to see us; to see how well they worked together on the yacht; to feel how much they loved their father and how they are becoming themselves — open, happy and joyful. I could see that I had put a seed in each of them by sharing my passion for the sea and the dolphins with them.

8

THE AWAKENED BRAIN

To enter into the perceptual world of whales and dolphins, you would have to change your primary sense from sight to sound. Your brain would process, synthesise, and store sound pictures rather than visual images.

Peter Warshall[1]

Our people believe that on the day we start communicating with dolphins and whales, great doors of knowledge and wisdom will be opened to us because these marine animals, the umkhoma [the conqueror] and the ihlengethwa [the redeemer] are custodians of knowledge that we wretched human beings have not dreamt about.

Credo Mutwa[2]

Measuring the 'dolphin effect' on people is not a simple task, especially because we strongly oppose any research which uses captive dolphins. It would have been much easier and more 'scientific' to have a dolphin in a pool, and compare results obtained from people who jump into the pool with those who don't (or who jump into a pool *without* a dolphin). It would have been much easier to control the parameters, to single out the dolphin effect.

In 1993, most dolphin researchers and therapists around the world were working with dolphins in captivity. At one stage some Australian dolphinaria were keen to have us as researchers, to help justify keeping their captive dolphins. We would never compromise our research into dolphin–human potential at the expense of the dolphins. That would be going against our *Declaration of Rights for Marine Mammals*.

The more we learn about dolphins, the more we appreciate how stressful and torturing captivity can be for them. Living with them in the wild, we see them constantly playing, making love, leaping, surfing, schooling and communicating. We see how much their lives rely on the pod, which includes their family and friends in a sophisticated society. We see the terrible conditions dolphins suffer in captivity, withdrawn from their playground and their community. And despite this, they will always cooperate with humans and support them.

Dolphins in captivity do not use sounds like they do in the wild. Researchers for a long time thought that dolphins stop using their sonar systems to avoid the stressful reverberations against the walls of a concrete pool, and hypothesised that they lose the ability to hunt for their food. More recent research shows that they probably stop using their echolocation simply and sadly because there is nothing to echolocate in their small and barren environment.

So, we conduct our research under far less 'scientific' conditions. We had to create new ways of researching. We currently use a number of instruments to measure the dolphin effect.

THE DOLPHIN WITHIN LOG

The Dolphin Within Log is a learning journal with four different parts. Participants like the log because it is often the first time they consider such questions about themselves. The log enables them to assess their life, to reflect on their past, present and future, and start exploring their dreams/vision/purpose. The four parts involve ticking boxes, colouring faces, drawings and writing.

The 'Colour your Face' exercise

This exercise is a mental check designed to be playful and powerful. It is a page of different faces, each associated with an adjective. Participants select and colour the faces that illustrate their daily life. Through this funny and quick assessment participants identify the emotions they usually feel during their daily lives, and those they have at the end of a Dolphin Within program. People are free to add faces and adjectives of their own. The results of this mental check show that 98% of the participants end up on the left side of the page, selecting adjectives like satisfied, joyful, happy, optimistic and confident. The other 2% select 'sad' and add, 'to leave the yacht and the pod'.

The Dolphin Within assessment

The second part of the Dolphin Within Log is a self-assessment questionnaire which measures ten dimensions: health and fitness, eating habits, fears or phobias, addictions, stress, creativity, relaxation techniques or spiritual practices, life purpose, love, relationships and environmental awareness.

At the beginning of the program, most participants have an average health and fitness level. They usually eat meat and drink alcohol, some smoke. They often suffer from stress over divorce/separation, death of a parent, work,

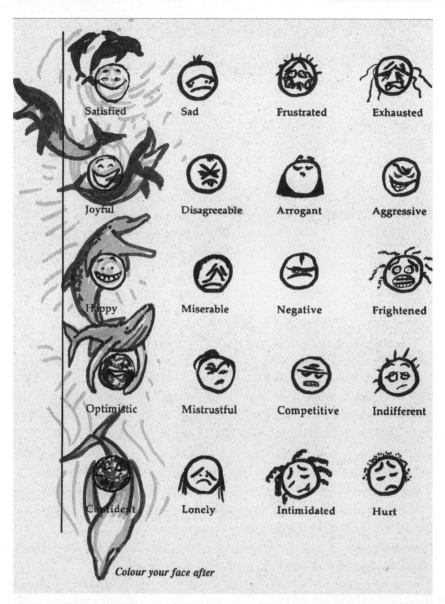

Satisfied   Sad   Frustrated   Exhausted

Joyful   Disagreeable   Arrogant   Aggressive

Happy   Miserable   Negative   Frightened

Optimistic   Mistrustful   Competitive   Indifferent

Confident   Lonely   Intimidated   Hurt

Colour your face after

retrenchment or mortgage and money concerns. The majority do not feel totally confident on a yacht or in the water, either due to fear of sharks or bad experiences in the past. Most do not use their full creativity, and do not practice relaxation or meditation techniques. They are usually not clear about their dream or purpose in life, and their relationships are not often totally fulfilled. They may have a religion, but few practice actively. Few people care strongly enough about the environment to practice recycling, or spend their time cleaning beaches or parks.

This typifies our average participants, but of course we have many outliers. We have vegetarians, artists and meditation practitioners who are active in environmental organisations and so on, but they don't represent the majority of our population.

The self-assessment questionnaire allows us to measure participants' progress months and years after their dolphin program. Many of them have changed jobs, they start to do things that they really enjoy, and they spend more time playing, relaxing or meditating. They start exploring their creativity through different classes or hobbies. They eat less meat, and some stop eating meat and even fish altogether. Several of them lose weight. Their stress levels decrease. They start to see their life situations (e.g. divorce, retrenchment) as opportunities to learn and grow. They become clearer about their purpose in life, and take more steps to bring their dreams into reality.

Many find renewed commitment in their existing relationships and a deeper sense of purpose in their partnership. Some become more actively involved in saving the environment in different ways.

Art therapy

Through art therapy, we assess the psychological health of participants. We ask participant to draw their lives to date before the swim. Then after the swim we ask them to draw their futures. The contrast between the colour, shape and content of the drawings illustrates the shift they have made. For example, Diane's drawings of her past and future are very powerful, encapsulating the transformation she went through. (See colour plates)

Before swimming with the dolphins, the picture is dark; the title is 'my past of Darkness'. The angles are straight with the wall and its bricks, the axe and the scene is in a rectangular box, a frame that looks like a cage. It describes a world of isolation, a broken heart, and a dangerous man with an axe. Diane has been attacked and hurt. She is a recluse behind a wall.

After swimming with dolphins, the picture is totally different, the colours are bright, the shapes are curvaceous, there are no straight lines and right angles. The scene is not framed or caged. The themes have completely changed: the little girl is now sailing a yacht, saved from the storm, sailing towards a happy home, under a beautiful rainbow. The tree is now full of life force and bright leaves.

We have collected hundreds of drawings where the colours in the pictures change from cold to warm, the lines from straight to curvaceous and themes from pain to happiness.

The personal journal

Everyone on the yacht is given a Personal Journal, in which they can write about their experiences. They have the choice to share them with us, either during the trip or in the months following.

Diane came to us with a lot of emotional pain, as we saw from her drawings. After the trip she wrote:

> I have many wonderful memories, for a change. I can now truly say that I am happy for the most part. When I do get depressed my thoughts return to the dolphin that swam close to me. The vision is very clear in my mind. I close my eyes and relive the experience. I feel more confident in my life. But mostly I feel relief to have lifted a heavy weight of pain from my heart.

Diane also wrote a poem about her experience:

Dolphin Magic

Lulled to peace in the arms of silence,
A hidden song flows like a stream.
Within the notes I know that I am here,
I know that I am whole.
The darkness within is splintered by the starfire jewel.
The angels of the sea appear to me in sanctuary.
I call to them for healing, I call to them for peace.
I feel their emotions, their essence, their joy.
And beyond the furthest reach I sense their presence.
A spell is cast.
The turmoil within is banished, my soul at peace.
Calmed by a love — so unique, so pure.
I look into the starfire jewel, the eye of the dolphin.
Our spirits have joined.

This poem inspired Ken Davis, who was on the yacht with Diane, to create an album of dolphin music which he called *Dolphin Magic*.

Naysa, a beautiful fourteen-year-old teenager from Chile, suffering after the divorce of her parents, wrote us the following.

> I want to thank you and William for everything. You, William and the trip have changed my outlook on life, I now see it differently, in a way that I never dreamt about or even seen before. The side of life where happiness, love and understanding could be felt at the same one time.
> Something I don't remember feeling in a long, long time, if ever. I might not have said much, but it was because I knew that I would not feel the same way for a long time, until I once again saw the ocean or something that represented it. I felt that time could not touch me. From morning till night my life was finally filled with something more than sadness and pain. The ocean to me is not only a large mass of moving

water, but something alive, full of wisdom and beauty, being surrounded by the ocean made me feel so free, so lucky just to have been able to see it. I hope that somewhere in the near future I can be once more board *Sirius*, which was filled with such security and overwhelming happiness.

Something that has also changed in my life is my 'huge' dream. I have no longer placed any limits on what I want to do. I no longer want to go to a place or two but all over the world. I want to travel, to see all the wonders of the world. Not only the beauty of the icebergs in Antarctica or the wonderful views from the moon and Mount Everest in the frontiers of Tibet and Nepal or the volcanic Mount of St Helen's and other snow/grass covered mountains but also the unknown ancient beauty of this world's unknown secrets of visitors from the 'heavens' found in Pyramids, temples and desert all over the world in places such as Peru, Rapa Nui, Mexico, Egypt and so many other places where secrets are just waiting to be revealed.

My life dream has expanded dramatically.

Perhaps dreams are made of lots of hard work. Perhaps if we try to cut corners we lose track of the reason we start dreaming and at the end we find that the dream no longer belongs to us. Perhaps if we just follow the wisdom from our hearts, then time will make sure we meet our destiny.

... is something that I have learnt.

The Dolphin Within Log, supplemented by our own observations and by video and photographic records of our trips, has allowed us to gather the information to identify the ten Dolphin Within patterns.

Later in the research program, we were able to add brainwave readings to help us describe the Dolphin Within experience more objectively.

NEUROFEEDBACK

For more than a year, I dreamt about having a machine to measure my brain after a dolphin experience. I knew that my whole being was 'zapped' by the dolphins' sounds, and I felt transformed. I had observed hundreds of people going through a similar experience. I was looking for a scientific language, to explain what was happening at the physiological and psychological levels.

The turning point in our research happened when we found the right equipment and got the finance (through many hours of consulting fees) to buy an electroencephalograph (a Neurodata 2000 EEG system), to monitor participants' brains before and after swims with dolphins. We then started our neurofeedback research.

Years ago, this kind of machine was enormous and only available in hospitals. Nowadays, thanks to modern technology, they fit into a small case and hook up to a notebook computer. With this system we can watch our brains on the screen, and receive feedback about any state we experience.

BRAINWAVE PATTERNS

Finding the EEG machine was a big step; learning to use it, to analyse and understand the data was even more exciting. I read many books on the brain, and I thank the dolphins for leading me to explore this fascinating field of human potential.

As is commonly known, we use very little of our brain's capacity; we have a lot to learn about unlocking the full potential of the brain.

The EEG, as the continuous 'roar' or 'noise' of the brain contains a fairly wide frequency spectrum, but it is not simply a hodgepodge of frequencies. Rhythmicity seems to create some law and order among waves of various lengths and amplitudes.

These frequencies are broken down into the following bands or ranges: Delta = below 3.5 cycles per second; Theta = 4–7.5 cycles per second; Alpha = 8–13 cycles per second; and Beta = above 13 cycles per second.

The sequence of these Greek letters is not logical and can be understood only in the historical view ... The terms 'alpha' and 'beta' rhythms or waves were introduced by Berger (1929). The term 'delta' rhythm was introduced by Walter (1936) to designate all frequencies below the alpha range. Walter himself, however found a need to introduce a special designation for the 4–7.5/sec range and use the letter theta ... to stand for thalamus because he presumed a thalamic origin of these waves.[3]

Research shows that during most of our normal daily activities, our brains produce electrical activity primarily in the beta frequency range (14–100 Hertz). This higher frequency is associated with action, focus, concentration and cognition. Beta helps us to deal with concrete, specific problems. However, too much beta can lead to stress, anxiety and burnout.

Alpha frequencies (8–13 Hertz) are associated with a relaxed, passive, unfocussed, calm and pleasant state. Many people produce more alpha simply by closing their eyes, unless they are too worried or stressed.

Theta frequencies (4–8 Hertz) are associated with what is often described as the 'twilight state' between waking and sleeping. It's difficult to maintain large amounts of theta without falling asleep. Theta brings unexpected dreamlike mental images, vivid memories, access to unconscious material, reverie, free association, sudden insight and creative ideas. It's a mysterious, elusive state.

> The normal adult waking record contains but a small amount of theta frequencies and no organised theta rhythm. Theta frequencies and theta rhythms, however, play an important role in infancy and childhood, as well in states of drowsiness and sleep ... the completed mature aspect of the human EEG cannot be expected before the age of 25—30 years.[4]

Brainwave patterns	Cycle/second (Hertz)	Natural purpose	Non-Meditators	Meditators
Beta	14 and over	fight flight freeze	normal	normal
Alpha	9–13	light sleep meditation	light sleep	light sleep or
Theta	4–8	light sleep meditation	deep sleep	deep sleep or
Delta	less than 4	deep sleep deep meditation	coma	coma or very

Brainwave patterns and associated states

Anxious or fearful states are associated with Beta EEG brainwave patterns which allow poor information flows between left and right hemispheres. It is not until we achieve the more relaxed Alpha rhythms, or preferably Theta brainwave patterns that we can more effectively process and clear the way to accessing the transpersonal levels of awareness.

W. Gray Walter (1959) has associated theta activity with emotional processes and thought that this activity might be a sign of 'relative maturity of the mechanisms linking the cortex, the thalamus and the hypothalamus'.[5]

People who meditate can reach alpha, theta or even delta states without been asleep, which means that they can process and access information that the average person can't. Accessing alpha and theta while conscious give the option to explore an alternative to the fight/flight/freeze reaction.

Rhythmical theta activity in the 6–7/sec range over the frontal midline region has been correlated with mental activities such as problem solving.[6]

CONTROL GROUP
Our control group consists of people who have the same experience in terms of swimming but without the presence of dolphins. We have also measured the brainwaves of participants in the dolphin program before and after a swim without dolphins, and then after a swim with the dolphins.

BRAIN RESEARCH PROTOCOL

We do two sets of readings — before and after people's dolphin experiences — and each reading comprises four minutes with eyes open followed by four minutes with eyes closed. When people close their eyes before the dolphin encounter, they relax and meditate if they have a technique of meditation. After the dolphin encounter, people close their eyes and recall the important images of the encounters, sounds and feelings.

Research shows that EEG activity varies when monitored from different locations on the head so we always use the same reference point, called P3 according to the International 10–20 system placement and letter-number designation.

Each case is analysed and put into the broader context of the life story of the individual. We have identified three patterns such as those illustrated by the following three examples.

LINDSAY: PRODUCTION OF THETA

Lindsay is an opera singer who works for a bank. He came with his new wife Angela. Lindsay's brain pattern showed a significant increase in alpha and theta after his swim. The dolphin experience gave him a taste of a new brain pattern.

His comments show that weeks after the trip, he was still able to re-access this brain pattern, or more precisely the state of consciousness indicated by it, any time he wanted, when he needed it.

What is interesting is that we have also tested people hours, days or weeks later, asking them to re-access their Dolphin Within state by going back to a memory of the weekend which was particularly strong for them, showing that the Dolphin Within state has a lasting effect.

It seems that because the brain has made a shift, participants can go back to that brainwave pattern at will. They can learn by practising to shift their brain states.

We have also seen that when we meet again as a pod in Sydney, far away from the dolphins, our brains shift into a theta state.

THETA TRAINING

The brainwave measurements showed us that the Dolphin Within patterns were associated with the *theta* state. Our next question was, what is the theta state? What does it have that is so particular? World brain research gives us more understanding.

Elmer and Alyce Green, from the Menninger Foundation in the United

States, were pioneers in brain research using EEGs. They measured the effects of training sessions to teach participants to produce more theta brainwaves. Their patients:

- Had vivid memories of long-forgotten childhood events.
- Became highly creative and had 'new and valid syntheses of ideas'.
- Fell in love, discovered new talents, decided to change jobs and strike out in new, more satisfying directions
- Felt their lives had been transformed.
- Became very healthy, with almost no illness whatsoever. Bringing 'physical healing, physical regeneration'.
- Experienced a new kind of body consciousness very much related to their total wellbeing.
- In the emotional domain, the theta state was 'manifested in improved relationships with other people as well as greater tolerance, understanding, and love of oneself and of one's world'.

Their results correlate well with our Dolphin Within patterns (Table 1).

The Dolphin Within program can be seen as an Alpha/Theta brainwave training, as participants learn to produce naturally more alpha and theta brainwaves, which have important therapeutic effects.

ALPHA AND THETA BRAINWAVE TRAINING

The use of alpha or theta brainwave neurofeedback therapy in the treatment of various disorders began with research in the 1960s and 1970s by people like Joe Kamiya and the Greens. Alpha brainwaves were said to be connected with feelings of wellbeing; theta brainwaves with the pre-sleep or day-dreaming state in which spontaneous imagery (or hypnagogia) arose; the beta brainwaves with concentration or anxiety and confusion; delta with sleep:

> It was speculated that levels of anxiety could be reduced, repressed psychological material could be processed and self-actualisation attained if the individual was trained via visual or auditory feedback to produce a higher percentage of higher amplitude of Alpha/Theta brainwaves.[7]

When in 1989, Drs Eugene Peniston and Paul Kulkosky's research was published, it created a major shift in the course of psychotherapy. As Dr Peniston described it a few years later:

> EEG biofeedback is being successfully utilised in the treatment of addictions, attention deficit disorder, post-traumatic stress, closed head

injury, epilepsy, and performance and learning development. Alpha-Theta brainwave training, a form of EEG feedback, provides a promising and effective new treatment for alcohol abuse, clinical depression, crack-cocaine abuse, chronic combat-related post-traumatic stress in Vietnam Veterans, multiple personality disorders and eating disorders.[8]

FREE FROM OLD SCRIPTS

In Nancy E. White's description of the Beta state (our usual daily state) as opposed to the Theta state (the Dolphin Within state), I can see many correlations with our Dolphin Within patterns.

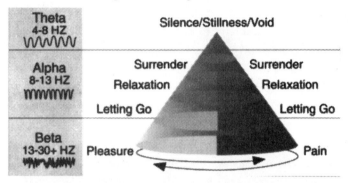

We live in a world that rewards the state of consciousness that I refer to as the 'beta state'. It is predominantly narrowly focused, rational, linear, a world dominated by the five senses. Sole reliance on this brain state inherently activates our ego self [selfishness] with its fears and anxieties, its need to be in control and to 'hold on'. We rock between pleasure and pain. Even when we are in the pleasure, we fear the loss of the pleasure, putting us back into the pain. But as we move our predominant brainwave frequency into lower realms, there is a surrender or 'letting go' of control.

As we go deeper, we disassociate from the brain/body system and often move into what might be called the 'Void'. It is in this silence between the thoughts where one can contact the hidden blueprint of intelligence and change it.[9]

CHILDHOOD MEMORIES AND THETA

One of the Dolphin Within patterns is access to unconscious material. This surfacing of memories from early childhood during the Dolphin Within program is again correlated with a theta state and can be understood as follows:

The highly emotional experiences of early childhood, and the (often mistaken) decisions which stem from them, are learned and stored as modifications of the slower background frequencies that were activated at that time.[10]

As children we are indeed in a theta-dominated world much of the time, up to the age of about six. The amount of theta progressively decreases as we grow into adulthood. Our childhood memories are state-dependent.

Research show that at four months of age, the dominant brain frequency is four cycles/sec, a theta state. At 12 months, it is 6c/sec, still a theta state. At three years old, children's brain frequency is 10c/sec, an alpha state. From age ten years onwards, there is a steady decline of slow frequencies.

To remember our childhood memories, we have to get back to the theta state in which they were first created, recorded or encoded.

Children spend most of their time in a trancelike, altered state of consciousness, highly conducive to learning; they are, like dolphins, operating in a theta state. This is why children and dolphins interact so easily; they operate on similar brainwave patterns. As adults with our beta brainwaves, we create noise for the dolphins. We can't relate to dolphins in the same way as children do, unless we learn from the dolphins' ways to re-enter the theta state or re-access our childlike state.

The Dolphin Within program allows some participants to enter a theta state that enables them to access more hurtful childhood memories stored in their subconscious. In the case of people who, like William, have suffered a traumatic event in relation to the sea (i.e., nearly drowning) when they were very young, the Dolphin Within program allows them to access the memory and reprogram a beautiful imprint of their new relationship with the sea.

Reaching a theta state can allow the inner child to be released.

> When we are injured physically or psychologically as a child we tend to develop mind defences which try to protect the child from further hurt. Each hurt changes the brain/mind and the defences become stronger. With enough trauma the inner child can be psychologically suffocated with layer after layer of defences. The true child (self) cannot be seen — it is buried under the trauma defences.[11]

The Dolphin Within experience finds its way through the defences by re-establishing the brain state (dominant EEG frequency) present at the time of the trauma, releasing the inner child. The result is an integration of early traumatic events in the present psyche of the adult.

Finding the Dolphin Within means finding the child or theta state of the child within. Opening this Pandora's Box is a very delicate and necessary process of transformation over the Dolphin Within program.

> The repository of our repressed traumatic memories has often been called Pandora's Box. Unfortunately, even though these hurtful memories are not available to our conscious mind and thus do not keep us in a

constantly angry or fearful state, they can still influence us in subtle and troublesome ways ... anything that in some way resembles the original trauma can cause one to feel anxious, uncomfortable, depressed or angry (without knowing why).[12]

I always say the Dolphin Within program aims at healing the participant's 'biggest pain'. If the repressed memories can be brought up through the experience with the dolphins and expressed through the different activities of drawing, journalising, talking around the camp fire or being in the water, their 'charge' can be dissipated as the material is integrated into their conscious mind. After this recovery and integration the traumatic memories will no longer bother them. Moreover, a significant amount of energy is no longer required for the repression. They feel better, more energetic, freer with emotions and no longer fearful of these stimuli.

A NEW SCRIPT

Research says that the natural shift in dominant brainwave frequencies during maturation could result in dysfunctional childhood learning being preserved in the unconscious.[13] To gain access to most of these 'state-bound' memories, one has to be in the state in which they were created, i.e. theta.

> As the subconscious appears to become more accessible in this deeply altered state, traumatic memories of the past are released and the subconscious seems more readily available to alteration or programming with new images.[14]

Dr Thomas Budzynski, a researcher and clinician, has found that theta is an ideal state for 'rescripting' or 'reimprinting' the brain, eliminating destructive behaviour or attitudes that are a result of scripts laid down in childhood (during times when the child is in a theta state) and replacing them with positive scripts.

The Dolphin Within program, viewed as alpha–theta training, is an interactive system of mind/brain, body, psyche and spirit. As we discharge negative emotions and rigidly held beliefs from our past wounds, our neurochemistry seems to be altered, our brainwaves are normalised and our psyche changes. Trauma is released and new, more desirable 'programs' are dropped into the deep unconscious.

After doing a PhD on scripts like this at 24, at last, ten years later, I found a way to deprogram the scripts, to write new ones.

SIMON: A CROSS-OVER POINT

A minority of subjects show an even more particular brain pattern than an increase of alpha and theta brainwaves.

Before his dolphin experience, Simon produced a lot of beta brain waves with his eyes open. He is a very successful, hardworking businessman. He didn't meditate, or practice any specific relaxation techniques. He arrived on the yacht with one, simple desire: to unwind. He didn't have any particular attraction to dolphins. His wife was the one fond of dolphins and that is why he was aboard *Sirius*.

If the brain can't slow down and produce more alpha and theta frequencies, individuals suffer from stress, anxiety and a lack of creativity in the long term. That is what many business people are indeed suffering from.

Simon interacted with the dolphins on the first day of the trip. He could distinctly hear them underwater. Overnight, while dolphins came around the yacht as we slept, he dreamt of a dolphin taking him by the finger to swim with him. The experience was very moving and touching for him. On Sunday, he had another swim and then went on the brainwave machine.

After the dolphin swim, Simon's brainwave pattern showed increased alpha, but what was even more remarkable was that he experienced an *alpha—theta crossover*. This occurs when the theta amplitude increases, and alpha recedes or diminishes, so theta supersedes alpha and the two reach the same amplitude.

Other researchers talk about 'miraculous resolutions' at the crossover point.[15] Dr Eugene Peniston, for example, shows that after thirteen months of training, an alpha—theta training group showed profound personality transformation, similar to those we see with the Dolphin Within effect. Their results correlate with our observations.

Peniston's Research

1. Significant increases in such qualities as warmth, abstract thinking, stability, conscientiousness, boldness, imaginativeness and self-control.
2. Significant decreases, not only in depression but also in anxiety.
3. Overcoming addiction.
4. Transforming personality.
5. Experiences of important, emotionally loaded, even life-transforming moments.
6. Creative insights, vivid memories from childhood, even spiritual moments.

The crossover point is described as 'the seemingly miraculous resolution of complex psychological problems'.

So, when we were wondering about miracles through the Dolphin Within program, especially in the case of Daniel and drug addiction, we were not so far out. When the human brain reaches that particular state, miracles are indeed possible!

KIRAN: AN 'AWAKENED MIND'

Like Simon, Kiran experienced a remarkable brainwave pattern after her dolphin experience. Kiran is a young woman who suffered from chronic fatigue syndrome for seven years. When she came on the yacht, it was the first time she had swum in the sea in four years. The dolphins were constantly next to her; at one point they stayed with her for an hour.

When we tested her brain afterwards, an unusual pattern was observed: beta, alpha, theta were all very high. This particular pattern is called in brain research the 'awakened mind'. It is an extraordinary brainwave pattern; large amounts of alpha and theta as well as strong beta and delta activity, all at the same time, combining the qualities of beta for alertness, arousal and concentration; alpha for relaxation; theta for memory, integrative experiences and healing, and delta for deep sleep, profound rest and release of growth hormones.

Her brain pattern showed that she was able to draw upon the relaxing, countering properties of the alpha state, the creative, memory-accessing properties of the theta state and the healing, 'grounding' properties of the delta state, whilst at the same time maintaining the alert concentration and external orientation of the beta state. This state of consciousness has been observed before; in Zen monks!

Six months later, she wrote '... a new outlook on life. A time of great happiness and joy to recall whenever I want. The Dolphin Within!'

The 'Dolphin Within' patterns that we have documented are integrative experiences which give feelings of psychological wellbeing with lasting effects. A lot of our participants change jobs or strike out in new, more satisfying directions. Their lives are transformed. They are psychologically healthier, they have more social poise, they are less rigid and conforming. They have more self-acceptance and creativity.

Such patterns, which might appear miraculous and magic, are scientifically validated and understandable when we measure participants' brains and find out that they are producing more theta, or experiencing an alpha—theta crossover, an awakened mind or transcendental patterns.

Human transformations are possible in such states of consciousness which are widely associated with access to stored memories, deeply internalised states, 'unheard or unseen things' coming to the surface, enhanced creativity, integrative experiences and psychological wellbeing.

THE HIERARCHY OF STATES

In order to explain the brain shift we have observed in our research, it is important to understand the hierarchy of states of consciousness. In their book *The Awakened Mind, Biofeedback and the Development of Higher States of Awareness,* Maxwell Cade and Nona Coxhead describe the following nine states in an ascending hierarchy from sleeping.[16] For the Sixth, Seventh and Eighth states, they found as many terms as there are philosophers and writers on the subject.

State 8   Cosmic Consciousness or Unity

State 7   Self-actualisation, Psychedelia, Illumination, Self-remembering and God Consciousness.

State 6   Creativity

State 5   Illumination, Cosmic Consciousness, The Awakened Mind

State 4   Meditation, Traditional Transcendental Consciousness

State 3   Waking, Waking Sleep

State 2   Hypnagogic State

State 1   Dreaming Sleep

State 0   Deep Sleep

Using this frame of reference, we can say that our research shows:

- Participants start the program in State 3 (Waking State) with dominant Beta.
- Participants from the control group without meditation training have either no change at all or easier access to the alpha brainwave. It is easier for them after a swim to stay still and quiet with closed eyes. They are more relaxed, the brain has slowed down, but we cannot say that their brain has shifted into State 4 with its associated alpha—theta brainwaves.
- Participants from the control group with meditation training (10%) can reach State 4 (Meditation) before and after the program.

 We found that many people who believed they were meditating were not really demonstrating an alpha—theta state. They achieved no more alpha plus beta than any untrained person who sits extremely still with closed eyes.
- 80% of the participants without meditation training reach State 4 (Meditation) with dominant alpha and peaks of theta. Participants with meditation training (10%) have easier and longer access to theta peaks.
- Participants who come twice or three times over the years have more and more easy access to the theta state.
- Among the 80% of participants with or without meditation training, 7% reach the alpha—theta crossover point, which means a point where theta takes over alpha.
- 10% of the participants reach State 5: the Awakened Mind.

The higher state of consciousness of the Awakened Mind has two main characteristics that Cade and Coxhead explain in their book:

1. The complete change which takes place in our sense of time, both in the timeless interval of the experience itself and in an altered attitude to time henceforward.
2. The absolute conviction of truth which these states convey; impossible though the individual may find it to express in words what he [she] has learned, he [she] has no doubt whatsoever of its truth. Our ordinary knowledge is obtained through the functions of the special senses and the reason, but mystical knowledge is direct and immediate knowledge, as opposed to indirect and mediate knowledge, intuitive knowledge rather than intellectual knowledge.

Basically, what is being transformed is one's level of awareness, not only of external reality but also of oneself. It is like gradually awakening from sleep and becoming more and more vividly aware of everyday reality.

I always challenged the participants who said at the end of the weekend: 'Now it's time to go back to reality'. I asked them why they didn't see their current 'dolphin' state as reality, and the other a state of illusion or sleepiness. In terms of brain research this is the case.

Our research shows participants entering the fifth state: the Awakened Mind. Beyond that Cade and Coxhead do not have a brain map. To our knowledge, no world research has a measurement, a physiological correlate or pattern; it is, for the present, beyond the machine.

The sixth state

Cade and Coxhead see the sixth state, Creativity, as the prime area of higher creative development, opening up and giving access to all the stored unformed material of all human consciousness (collective unconscious of Carl Jung). They have observed it with subjects who frequently experience State 5, those who meditate as a way of life, those who spend a great deal of their time in some highly creative pursuit. They also note that creativity may appear at the hypnagogic level in reverie too.

Albert Einstein, unquestionably one of the greatest creative geniuses of recent centuries, appeared to live in a semipermanent alpha state. Electroencephalographic studies showed that, quite unlike most people Einstein could maintain continuous high-amplitude alpha while solving complex mathematical problems in his head.[17]

The seventh state

Cade and Coxhead's description of the seventh state (self-actualisation) fits with William's and my personal transformation and some of the participants of the Dolphin Within programs. However, we cannot say — yet — that we are reaching that state as we do not yet have a brain map. We can say that the Dolphin Within program is a gateway towards that state.

The self-actualising human is one who is:

a) sufficiently free from illness;
b) sufficiently gratified in his or her basic needs, positively using his or her talents and capacities;
c) motivated by some values which he or she strives for and to which he or she is loyal.

All self-actualising people are devoted to some task, call, vocation or beloved work. 'The devotion and dedication is so marked that one can fairly use the old words calling, vocation or mission to describe their passionate, selfless, and profound feeling for their "work".' We could even use the words destiny or 'fate'.

Self-actualising people have a strong sense of their good fortune in this ideal situation, of luck, of grace, of awe that this miracle should have happened, or wonder that they should have been chosen.

At this level, the division of work and play is transcended.

The Dolphin Within program can be seen as a process which leads to self-actualised personalities. In *On Becoming a Person*, Carl Rogers sees self-actualised personalities moving in the direction of the following goals:[18]

- Increased openness to life and experience, with reduction in defensiveness.
- Increased interest in the here-and-now; living in the present moment.
- Increased awareness of both the internal and the external aspects of each new experience.

Finally, using the terms of psychologist J. C. Gowan, the Dolphin Within experience can develop the characteristics of: openness to life and experience; creativeness; integration, wholeness, unity of the personality; firm identity, autonomy, inner-guidance; great awareness, both internal and external; spontaneity, expressiveness, aliveness; detachment, objectivity; ability to love; and clear, efficient perception of reality — no illusions.

The eighth state

The eighth state is known generally as cosmic consciousness. Cade and Coxhead describe the experience of Dr Bucke, who had a classical 'mystical illumination' and listed in his book *Cosmic Consciousness* the following as characteristic of 'the supreme experience':

- An awareness of intense light.
- The individual seems bathed in an emotion of joy, assurance, triumph, 'salvation'.
- An intellectual illumination quite impossible to describe. In an intuitive flash, the awareness of the meaning and drift of the universe, an identification and merging with creation.
- A sense of immortality.
- The fear of death falls off like an old cloak — not, however as a result of reasoning — it simply vanishes.
- Loss of the sense of sin.
- Subsequently there is a charismatic change in personality.

I can relate to such descriptions. Not all of my dolphin encounters have created such states, but some have. Again, I don't have any brain reading patterns to show that state — the machine is not sophisticated enough. I just know that that is where the dolphins help me to go. I am interested in receiving feedback from readers who can tell me where their experiences fit in relation to the higher states.

SELF-REGULATING OUR BRAINS

The Dolphin Within state therefore has many therapeutic effects; most people show an increase of alpha and theta brainwaves, entering State 4, while a small group enter State 5, the Awakened Mind.

As we use the electroencephalograph for the research, participants can also learn with the machine to re-access the state and train themselves to produce more alpha—theta brainwaves.

Whatever frequencies it goes into, the brain experiences a state that is often new to the participant. Importantly, once the brain has reached this new state, it is possible to learn how to access it at will. That's why Diane found that, when she feels low, she just has to think about dolphins, to go back to her memory of the trip, and she immediately feels high again.

What I suggest is that people who have a Dolphin Within experience are in fact imprinting in their memories a new state of consciousness, one that helps them to de-stress or focus, depending on what they need. Their brains find new ways to operate. They thus become more able to regulate their brains, to produce as an act of will the brain frequencies they need, whenever they need them.

The Dolphin Within program could thus been seen as a form of accelerated, natural transpersonal training. To reach a state of transpersonal beingness and creativity, one has to still the body, the emotions and the mind while remaining conscious, open to the creativity inside; this is not an easy task.

The Dolphin Within program is an effective and efficient way of approaching this state, with significant benefits: improved physical functioning, emotional stability, sharpened thinking, and true creativity — 'the solution of insoluble problems in unpredictable ways'.

Beyond theta, the personal unconscious, beyond the dissociative state, is the state called transcendence: individuals move beyond their personal egos, beyond their personal unconscious minds, into a peak state of universal awareness.

> Experiences in this state are many times ineffable and cannot be explained or described in words. Experiences in this realm are more than passive diversions. Their creative power can change the very nature of the participants' reality.[19]

DOLPHINS: CATALYSTS FOR HUMAN TRANSFORMATION

The pattern emerging from our observations was becoming clear; dolphins are catalysts for a human self-transformation process. Being in their presence, being in the water with them, being in their world of sound activates energy within us which seems to unlock our self-healing power, bringing physiological, psychological and spiritual transformation.

Our research indicates that the Dolphin Within experience supports us to use our brains better, to extend human consciousness and to explore our full potential. The introduction of the EEG as part of our assessment process has brought new light to our understanding of Dolphin-assisted Therapy. It also provides the means, through biofeedback, to learn how to reproduce the state of consciousness that the dolphins' ultrasonic frequency puts us into.

One may think that our research helps to demystify the healing power of dolphins. I still think that there is much more to learn, and that we are just at the beginning of an exploration of human consciousness in contact with dolphins.

ECHOLOCATION THERAPY

Having shown that the brain shifts following a Dolphin Within experience, the next question is, how does it happen?

I have personally experienced, for four years now, the dolphins' sounds scanning my body. Participants who swim with us report the same feeling. My hypothesis is that it is the sounds of the dolphins that help us to shift our brains.

Dolphins use sounds to see or echolocate. They have physical eyes, but through sound they have a much more sophisticated eye to perceive. They send a sound, and from the reflection they receive back, they 'see' objects outside and inside, like an X-ray or a holographic picture. They send and receive sounds across the range of 100-150 000 Hz, while we hear over a much more limited range of 20-20 000 Hz. While we cannot hear the whole range of dolphin sounds, we can feel them throughout our bodies.

SOUND THERAPY

One explanation of the dolphin healing could be that the sound might remind us of perhaps the most powerful and evocative sound; that of the rhythmic booming of blood through our ears as we rest inside our mothers before birth.

Alfred Tomatis, a French medical doctor, found that brain development is influenced by the sounds we experience while in the womb. When we are in amniotic fluid, because the sound travels through water five times more efficiently than through air, our sense of hearing is five times more acute.

Tomatis waterproofed microphones and speakers and submerged them in water to record and produce the type of sounds infants hear, filtered through the amniotic fluid. These are the sounds of the mother's pulse, respiration, voice, intestines, heart and all sounds of the external world, filtered through the mother's belly. Tomatis found that these sounds were predominantly high-pitched squeaks, hisses, swishes and whistles, in the frequency range above 88 000 Hz.

These sounds are well outside our normal range of hearing, but are within the range of sounds produced by dolphins. That means that we may have another correlation between Tomatis' research and ours in terms of sound therapy.[20]

When Tomatis played his recorded sounds to children with learning disabilities, autism, dyslexia, hyperactivity and so on, he noticed dramatic improvements in learning and behaviour. The sounds 'awaken a sense of our most archaic relationship with the mother'. They seemed to boost brainpower, energise the body and reduce stress-related problems of all sorts.

Sounds have an impact on the brain. The ear not only hears, but receives vibration waves at other frequencies which stimulate sensory nerves in the inner ear, where they are transformed into electrical impulse that travel along several routes to the brain. Insufficient exposure to high frequency sound ranges can have a similar effect to insufficient nutrients, depleting our resources and leading to sickness.

Research shows that, whilst most of us are born with the ability to hear sound waves between 20 and 20 000 Hz, noise pollution and physical and psychological stress have dramatically diminished the hearing range of most people. In a way, many people in our modern society have become deaf to the energising, healing nutrients of these sounds. They are, in a real sense, in a state of sound deprivation.

This has an effect on the voice too. The voice indeed can only produce what the ear can hear, within a narrow range between 300 and 3000 Hz. When the ears are 'opened' by high-frequency sound, they produce a whole-body healing and energising effect, a dramatic increase in mental powers and a noticeable opening and enriching of the vocal range.*

Tomatis' research is important for our planned Dolphin Therapy centres, which will reproduce the Dolphin Within experience without the physical presence of dolphins. It shows that the technology is available.

FROM *HOMO LIMBUS* TO *HOMO THALAMUS*

Researchers say that there are two activation centres in the brain, one being the emotionally activating limbic system, the other being the thalamo-cortical system, responsible for organising cognitive function.

The limbic system is the older, reptilian part of the brain, from which originate the primitive emotions, rage, fear, anxiety etc. The reptilian, primitive brain still controls the world, generating hate, wars, greed, repression, control and terror. As humans, we are still dominated by the limbic brain.

By contrast, the thalamic system is responsible for the overall management of the higher brain centres and the cortex.

By experiencing the Dolphin Within, we discover and develop our brains. The dolphins might help us to go from *Homo limbus* to *Homo thalamus*. Reducing the dominance of the limbic system will allow the next phase of our evolution to proceed.

Evolution has produced the 'fight or flight' reactions as a protective mechanism. The Dolphin Within experience helps us develop a third way, not a reaction but a response, the dolphin way: the play.

DOLPHIN WITHIN THERAPY

Through our research we have explored and developed a new therapy involving wild dolphins as catalysts for human transformation. The Dolphin

---

* Since these sounds are partially outside the human hearing range, they can be played on tapes or CDs as silent background to music. A brain stimulating effect without even being audible.

Within therapy is more than a swimming program with dolphins. It is an integrated program based on an oceanic adventure, art therapy, group therapy and neurofeedback therapy, in which the encounters with the dolphins play an important part. It has the following applications.

Tuning into stored traumas

Some participants, when shifting into different brainwave frequencies, experience discomfort, anxiety and nausea, followed by a release of traumatic material and then peace. The Dolphin Within state thus accesses specific traumatic events that are coded and stored in the brain according to specific frequencies.

Releasing physical pain

Wilhelm Reich pointed out that traumatic experiences are stored away in the body as habitual muscular tensions and neuromuscular patterns he called 'body armour'. We store away traumas by coding them with brain-wave frequencies and then 'protecting' ourselves from those stored traumas by rigidly keeping ourselves from re-entering those regions.

Reich asserted that early imprints and scripts inhibiting the expression of free energies create rigidity and blockages that are anchored in the body as armour and these tensions are the causes of physical and metal illness.

By learning to return through the Dolphin Within experience to the original state in which the script was laid down, participants are able to access and release many of the rigid, root causes of illness.

Ending addiction and substance abuse

Addictive behaviour patterns such as smoking, overeating and compulsive gambling bring extremely high levels of arousability — addicts are more sensitive than most people. High levels of rapid beta brainwave activity and low realisation of alpha and theta are typical.[21]

Addiction to a substance emerges from changes in our mind–body 'reward system' and results in changes in our abilities to experience pleasure. Nothing is fun because the brain has lost its ability to experience fun.

The Dolphin Within frequencies are a return to fun. Participants can experience pleasure and fun again naturally with the dolphins, and restore the pleasure-producing neurochemicals. Happiness then lies not outside the body, but within.

Anxiety

Typical external signs of anxiety are: sweaty palms, a tight chest, pounding heart, butterflies in the stomach, restlessness, irritability, trembling hands and a feeling of being out of control. The threat is internally created by potential or future events. Participants usually switch off the fight or flight response, which blocks their ability to feel fear altogether.

Dolphin Within participants no longer experience a 'fight or flight' reaction, but a flow response, a relaxation response; the dolphin way.

Depression

If anxiety is the self-generated fight-or-flight response, depression seems to be the acceptance that neither fight nor flight is a possible option. The Dolphin Within state can produce more brainwave activity across the whole spectrum. It seems to help boost the brain out of its depressed, playing possum response to produce permanent changes, because participants can re-access this new brain pattern.

Phobias

Phobic reactions seem to result from conditioning. Through the Dolphin Within experience, participants suffering from phobia of water, sharks, seasickness and so on move through the levels of increasing exposure to the phobia while remaining calm and relaxed, becoming progressively desensitised.

Peak health

The Dolphin Within state is a state for supercharging our immune system. Our body's homeostatic or self-healing mechanisms work most effectively when we are relaxed.

Personality transformation

Our observations show that participants demonstrate, both on the yacht and also months or years after, increased warmth, abstract thinking, stability, conscientiousness, boldness, imaginativeness and self-control. Some talk about a state of peace, of connection with spiritual worlds.

NEW FRONTIERS

What are the new frontiers we want to explore on the brain research side? We continue with the brainwave readings, gathering more observations and statistical information. One day it will be possible to monitor peoples' brains while they are swimming with the dolphins, not just before and after the encounters. The electrode will be waterproof and the information will be radio-transmitted to the computer. The technology is available, it is just a question of getting the finance.

In exploring the healing power of dolphins, our research seeks an understanding of how the ultrasound frequencies that dolphins emit (and that we cannot hear) help us to shift into brain patterns that we have never explored before. If individuals who have never meditated nor learnt relaxation techniques can learn how to self-regulate their brains by accessing states that a yogi might start to experience only after many years of practice, the prospect of an accelerated program to realise full human potential is quite plausible. Our research raises questions in terms of understanding more of the effects and of the ultrasound frequencies the dolphins are sending.

REFERENCES

1 Peter Warshall, 'The Ways of the Whales' in *Mind in the Water*, Joan MacIntyre (ed.), Sierra Club Books, San Francisco, 1974.

2 Credo Mutwa, *ISILWANE, the Animal, Tales and Fables of Africa*. Struik Publishers, Cape Town, 1996.

3 Ernst Niedermeyer, *The Normal EEG of the Waking Adult. Electroencephalography, Basic Principles, Clinical Applications, and Related Fields*. Williams & Wilkins, Baltimore, 1993.

4 ibid.

5 V. J. Walter and W. G. Walter, The central effects of rhythmic sensory stimulation. *Electroencephalography and Clinical Neurophysiology* 1949; 1: 57-86.

6 A. P. Arellano and R. S. Schwab, Scalp and basal recording during mental activity. *Proceedings of the 1st International Congress of Psychiatry, Paris, 1950.*

7 Eugene G. Peniston, EEG alpha–theta neurofeedback: promising clinical approach for future psychotherapy and medicine. *Megabrain Report* Volume 2, Number 4, 1994.

8 ibid.

9 Nancy E. White, Alpha-theta training for chronic trauma disorder, a new perspective. *Megabrain Report*. Volume 2, Number 4, 1994.

10 J. Cowan, Alpha-theta brainwave biofeedback: the many possible theoretical reasons for its success. *Biofeedback* 1993; 21(2): 11-16.

11 Thomas H. Budzynski, The new frontier. *Megabrain Report* Volume 2, Number 4, 1994.

12 ibid.

13 W. Beckwith, Addiction, transformation and brainwave patterns. *Megabrain Report*. Volume 1, Number 3, 1992.

14 White, op. cit.

15 Eugene Peniston and Paul Kulkosky, Alpha-theta training and beta-endorphin levels in alcoholics. *Alcoholism: Clinical and Experimental Research* 1989; 13: 271-279.

16 C. Maxwell Cade and Nona Coxhead, *The Awakened Mind, Biofeedback and the Development of Higher States of Awareness.* Delacorte Press, New York, 1979.

17 ibid.

18 Carl Rogers, *On Becoming a Person.*

19 White, op. cit.

20 Alfred Tomatis, *The Conscious Ear,* Station Hill Press, Barington, New York, 1991.

21 Michael Hutchison, *Megabrain Report* Volume 2, Number 4, 1994.

9

THE ENERGY FIELD

When Carl Jung was asked if he believed in spiritual beings that transcended the limits of time and space, he said, 'I don't believe. I know.'

The aim of our research with the dolphins is to understand what happens to people in contact with the dolphins, so that we can reproduce it without the participation of the dolphins. After all, we cannot impose pressure on the dolphins, even if we find out that they are helping us to get in touch with our full potential!

PUZZLING EXPERIENCES

We know now that the brain switches from a beta state to a theta state, leading to an alpha—theta crossover or an 'awakened mind', indicating a clear shift in consciousness that has therapeutic effects. Brain research is one scientific way to look at the phenomenon, and it provides fascinating results. If we want to reproduce the Dolphin Within experience, we need to create an environment and a process that allows participants to shift their brains into a theta state, into an 'awakened mind'.

However, a Dolphin Within experience is more than a brain shift; participants report observations that still leave us puzzled. Our method is to explore the Dolphin Within phenomenon from different angles, to make links between different fields of research. So, what are the experiences that still trigger our curiosity?

'Feeling zapped'

Many participants report feeling a vibration throughout the body. People use the words 'feeling zapped' or feeling a 'tingling'. Dolphins' sounds go beyond physical sounds; we cannot hear them, but we feel their effects. Some participants, like Lindsay and William, also report feeling a flash of light. Lindsay said: 'I was on the rope with the dolphins around me; I went into my third eye and I received a flash of light'.

On one occasion, William was snorkelling with a wet suit with a hood, in winter. He didn't hear the dolphins coming next to him, and he later reported: 'I suddenly felt a rush of light, and a kind of explosion in my heart'.

Another time, as William was holding onto the end of the rope behind the boat, surrounded by dolphins: 'I was holding the rope by just two fingers. My whole body was relaxed and totally free of thoughts and tension. There was not one muscle tense beyond my two fingers. I then suddenly felt a spring of light coming out of my scalp. I felt that I knew what it meant to be a dolphin'.

How should we interpret these experiences?

THE FIELD OF ENERGY

Newtonian physics of the early 18th century, with its definition of the universe as being made of solid objects, and humans only having a physical body, has been questioned more and more by new discoveries. By the early 19th century, the discovery and investigation of electromagnetic phenomena had already led to the concept of an energy field: a condition in space that has the potential to produce a force.

In the 1940s, a Professor of Anatomy at Yale University Medical School, Harold Saxton Burr, discovered that humans, animals, trees and plants have electrodynamic fields around their physical bodies. He called these fields bioelectrical or L fields — the fields of life. Burr proved that emotions affect these life fields.[1]

THE LIFE FORCE

For over 5000 years, mystics from all parts of the world have been describing — in their own words, through their traditions — many things that scientists have observed only recently.

Ancient Indian spiritual tradition talks of a universal energy called *Prana* as the basic constituent and source of all life. Yogic practice aims at moving this energy through breathing techniques, meditation and physical exercise in order to maintain altered states of consciousness.

As long as five thousand years ago, the Chinese believed in the existence of *Qi,* the vital energy. Traditional Chinese acupuncture is based on balancing the circulation of this energy in the body.

Christian religious paintings often portray Jesus and other holy people surrounded by fields of light. Many esoteric teachings from the ancient Hindu Vedic texts, the Theosophists, the Rosicrucians, the Native American Medicine People, the Tibetan and Indian Buddhists, the Japanese Zen to Rudolph Steiner describe this 'human energy field' in detail.

A MODEL OF SUBTLE BODIES

If we want to explore the Dolphin Within state further, we need a model of subtle bodies which relates to experiences, perceptions, and phenomena that we observe today, including the 'energy field'. According to the following simple model,[2] which encompasses the body, mind and spirit and fits with both western and eastern traditions of philosophy, a person can be regarded as made of four parts:

1. A Physical Body.
2. An Etheric Body, or layer of life force; the Indian *Prana* or Chinese *Qi*.
3. An Astral Body, or layer of mental consciousness: emotions and thoughts.
4. The Higher Self: facets of the divine side of the human nature.

What people report as 'zapping' from dolphins is an etheric sensation. Vibration is equated to etheric energy, to life force. It seems important to learn to manage the health of the etheric body as well as the physical one.

> The stress of modern life tends to generate a cramped condition in which the astral body never really lets go of its grip on the etheric. In the long run this creates a wearing out and an exhaustion of the etheric layer ...
>   The accumulation of negative energies in the etheric body of the majority of the population contributes greatly to the general 'malaise' and the level of neurosis of the modern world. The proper functioning of the physical body depends to a great extent on the right flow and balance of the circulations of the etheric body.[3]

To maintain our life force, the health of the etheric body, there have to be times when it can completely relax. The more the grasp of the astral body is released, the more the etheric body is free to relax and expand. It is this etheric–astral interface and the management of it that is at the root of many human conditions.

How can we relax, clean, balance the circulation of the etheric body?

> It is said that the physical body is to the earth element, the astral body to the air element, the Ego to the fire element and the etheric body to the water element.[4]

With this background on subtle bodies, we can describe aspects of the Dolphin Within experience as follows:

1. Being in water, the physical body is in a gravity-free environment (especially when the body is supported by a wetsuit).
2. When people are towed along on the dolphin rope (while the yacht is moving), their etheric body is cleansed of any negative energy and the

astral body becomes quieter (emotions and thoughts decrease).

3. When surrounded by dolphin sounds in the water, the etheric/astral interface is loosened.

4. Being lost in a different world of sounds allows the ego/higher self to shine through.

A Dolphin Within experience, like any deep experience, changes the nature of the relationship between the astral and etheric. A Dolphin Within experience seems to change the nature of our make-up, and brings our higher self closer.

From the astrally charged pleasure and pain state (characterised by beta brainwaves), we experience a release, a loosening of the grip of the astral on the etheric, and we enter a more relaxed state (alpha and theta brainwaves). We experience the higher self more directly and consciously, and a more fundamental connection between the self and the physical is experienced, instead of through the astral—etheric grasping.

Lindsay was on the dolphin rope for half and hour: 'It was like being in space, I could see stars ... It was like a shock to come back on the yacht'. It is the astral body coming back into the etheric body, which clashes. In a way, he was re-experiencing the incarnation process.

From our research we can say that our present understanding, using the model of subtle bodies, is as follows:

> The Dolphin Within experience, combining as it does the aquatic environment with specific ultra-sonic frequencies which shift the brain into an 'awakened mind', allows the disconnection of the astral body (emotions and thoughts), awakens and expands the etheric body (life force) and allows the higher self to shine through. The Dolphin Within state is equivalent to a direct connection with the higher self.

Bear in mind that every day adds more information and observations, and more knowledge to our research.

A Dolphin Within experience could be like a shortcut in our evolutionary path. It is an altered state of consciousness which puts us directly in touch which our full potential, our higher self.

What we call *dolphin drunkenness* is the capacity to be intoxicated without the need for any external substance. Living in the Dolphin Within state is to be permanently intoxicated with spirit, with what we receive from the connection between our higher self, the planet and the universe. Being in the Dolphin Within state means to be instantly high.

Such experiences are much sweeter than chocolate or drugs. When we feel alive, feel the spirit of life, we have the absolute high. Because our life becomes full of peace, joy and spirit, it feels strange to watch people driving themselves on cigarettes, alcohol, materialism, to search outside for what is already waiting for them inside: the Dolphin Within.

DEVELOPING YOUR DOLPHIN WITHIN STATE

In *The Centre of the Cyclone,* John Lilly wrote: 'It is my firm belief that the experience of higher states of consciousness is necessary for survival of the human species'.[5]

You might ask, how can I experience this state? You can join us on a Dolphin Within trip of course, or go on a dolphin swim program close to where you live. However, we are aware that not everyone can do this, even if you can join us on the Internet. We may yet develop a Dolphin Within experience through virtual reality — available on the Internet or CD-ROM.

Learning to meditate would be a way to experience a higher state of consciousness. There are ways to have a little taste of the Dolphin Within state, by following the simple guidelines below. Please practise and share your discoveries with us.

The power of water and breath holding

The best and quickest way to cleanse the etheric body is to be in water. So showers, baths, spas, where you consciously release your negative energies and recharge are recommended. However, doing it in cold water, and putting your head underwater, is even more beneficial. As soon as people put their heads under water, the heart rate slows down. This is well known among scuba divers as the 'mammalian diving reflex effect'. It is found in diving mammals such as whales, dolphins, seals and humans. This bradycardia, or slowing of the heart, is an involuntary response found in breath-hold diving. It reduces the circulation but does not reduce the oxygen consumption. It is triggered by cold moisture in contact with the face, but what causes the resulting decline in heart rate is not fully understood. Breath-holding normally increases the heart rate. So swimming and putting your head under water has a more beneficial effect than just being in a bath.

Swimming in the ocean or a river has fantastic therapeutic effects. I follow the daily practice of meeting Bluey the blue groper and his friends. I enter the dolphins' world by going snorkelling and practising my dolphin swim. I also practise breath retention underwater, as I want to stay a long time with the fish. When I come out I feel alive, cleansed and ready to face anything.

A Russian respiratory physician, Professor Buteyko, has provided a physiological explanation for this sensation. According to Buteyko, many of us typically breath in too great a volume of air for our body's needs (hyperventilation) and consequently breath off carbon dioxide too rapidly for the lungs to maintain the right level of this gas in the air sacs. When carbon dioxide is too low it causes a chemical reaction which makes it hard for oxygen to be released from the blood stream into the tissues of the body which then become starved of oxygen. An organic system starved of oxygen cannot be healthy. Symptoms of over breathing can include viral illnesses, allergies and asthma. To break this cycle, Buteyko advocates the specialised technique of breath retention — precisely the sort of respiration that occurs quite naturally when diving.[6]

I go snorkelling every day at 7 a.m. I meet a whole community of older people who have followed this ritual for most of their lives. On every Sydney beach, there is a group of people, mostly men (seemingly with an average age of seventy), who always start their day with a swim. Every day I feel I am watching a scene from the film *Cocoon,* when old people jump in the water, start laughing and come out more alive and younger-looking. These Australians have the secret of long life. I have a special place in my heart for one of them, who suffers from chronic arthritis and can't really walk. I often help him on the steps. As soon he reaches the water, he jumps in like a twenty-year-old, and swims like a fish.

Snorkelling and scuba diving
Snorkelling and scuba diving are fantastic ways to enter the dolphin world, which I highly recommend. On our Dolphin Within trips we give people the opportunity to discover for the first time this other world, through introductory snorkelling and dive sessions.

Snorkelling means breath retention when you go down to see a dolphin. This has a powerful effect. Indeed, there are several meditation techniques based on breath retention. However, when you do it while snorkelling it is so easy because you are fascinated by the beauty of the ocean, its fauna and flora, so you stay longer.

I always knew from experience that diving was producing an important therapeutic effect on the brain. All scuba divers will tell you that when you come out after a dive you feel peaceful and calm; any stress is gone. My research on the brain led me to read an article on diving and EEG patterns that confirmed my intuition. The EEG alterations from diving are increased alpha and theta frequency activity.[7]

Diving could be seen as a therapy, or a way to explored altered states of consciousness. It is certainly a quick way to go inside and become more in touch with the inner self.

The Belgian Dr Karl Ringoet, who is both a psychoanalyst and a diving instructor, claimed to have cured schizophrenics by using a strange combination of scuba diving and psychoanalysis.[8] I think that we have a lot to discover about what the ocean can give us in terms of healing.

Improvising

For people who do not have access to this other world every day, I am aware that we need to create other ways. I recommend that you create your own program, using the resources at your disposal. The more you can recreate the Dolphin Within experience, the better.

First of all, you need a dolphin space. I have painted a whole room in blue with dolphins. I am not an artist, but I created my dolphin space in one afternoon and everyone loves it. It is very important to have your space.

Use blue or turquoise paint. Colour therapy says that they induce a sense of calm. In my experience there is a certain blue—emerald, which is really a dolphin colour. That is the one I used in my dolphin room; Howie Cooke often uses it too, in his paintings.

You can create a dolphin space anywhere. Your bath or jacuzzi might be the place where you enter the dolphin world. Did you know that Candido Jacuzzi, an Italian living in California, was an expert in fluid dynamics. He invented the whirlpool bath to treat his grandson, who suffered from rheumatoid arthritis.

Try to avoid electrical light; sun, daylight and candles are much better.

The first Dolphin Healing Centre in the world is in Kyoto, Japan. A Japanese couple runs it in a temple. They use large dolphin posters and videos.

Dolphin ways to connect

Select your dolphin photos, posters and paintings. Something which really attracts you. I don't really like plastic or commercial artefacts based on dolphins. That is why the Society promotes artists inspired by dolphins to create artistic jewellery, posters, sculptures, paintings and so on. Sometimes you see a dolphin that doesn't look like a dolphin. When you see Howie's paintings, you can feel that he has spent his life with dolphins and whales. I have dolphin T-shirts and a dolphin ring which are important for me.

Create your own drawing, painting or artwork. The key is what is important for you, not your artistic capabilities but your sense of the artistic.

Watch a dolphin video. We have built up a collection of beautiful dolphin and whale video films that uplift you just by watching them.

Practise

Listen, watch the dolphins and start resonating with them. One important principle of the Dolphin Within approach is that it is not about visualisation. It is better if you don't try to visualise or imagine anything, because that is the work of the mind (beta brainwaves). Your aim is to slow down your brain, into theta. Just let it happen, if images, lights, flashbacks or anything come into your vision, that's fine. But don't make them up, don't try to induce them. Don't actively visualise any pattern into your field of consciousness.

If nothing happens, it's fine not to rush or to try too hard. The idea is to start being a dolphin, feeling their power and softness and seeing the world the way they see it.

- Look at a photo, a film, a painting, a sculpture
- Then close your eyes
- Focus on your sonar: third eye, the space between your eyebrows
- Listen to the dolphins' sounds
- Produce sounds yourself, very high-pitched sounds
- Imagine yourself swimming like a dolphin
- Feel, listen to, smell, touch, see and more importantly perceive the dolphins from within.

THE FIGHT OR FLIGHT REACTION

Get into your Dolphin Within state, especially when you are on the edge of reacting as a Shark! What is the 'natural' reaction when the life of a human being is in danger? It is the 'fight or flight' reaction, mediated through a massive discharge of adrenalin, triggered by the sympathetic nervous system. Arterial blood pressure increases, the heart beats faster and more strongly and a number of drastic physiological changes take place that increase your muscular strength and mental activity. Suddenly, you are fully awake.

What does this mean in terms of subtle bodies? The astral body pulls strongly into the etheric and physical bodies and exerts its action, which tends to make everything contract.

In order to get out of the fight or flight reaction, you need to practise the Dolphin Within state. The more you practise, the easier it becomes. The astral body (layer of mental consciousness and emotions) is floating, away from the etheric and physical body, you are asleep, sleepy or in a deep state of meditation. Everything in the physical body is very relaxed and the etheric body is dilated and spread out to a certain extent.

Before an event where you need access to your whole potential, switch your brain to a memory of a dolphin encounter, or to a film or photo which has created a powerful emotion in you. I have learnt how to access this state at any time, as illustrated by the following story.

Cigarette butts

When we arrived at The Anchorage one Friday night as usual for our Dolphin Within weekend, I walked along the jetty and discovered that a game fishing competition was going on that weekend. A group of ten Australian game fishermen had their big boats moored next to *Sirius*. They were having a good night, drinking, smoking and talking loudly.

The Anchorage is the best marina I have seen; it is very quiet and private and dolphins often come into the marina itself. I usually sleep on the deck of *Sirius*, and I am often awakened in the night by them.

As I walked past the boats and the men, I noticed all the cigarette butts floating in the water at their feet. My love of dolphins would not let me enjoy my night and let the pollution happen, without saying something. I left the trolley of gear next to *Sirius* and went back to join the group of drinking fishermen. I gently explained to them that the marina is like a reserve, that dolphins come at night and that cigarette butts can kill dolphins and turtles ... and it would be great if they could use an ashtray.

They reacted violently. Under the effect of the alcohol, they didn't want to have a young blonde telling them what to do. They asked me where my strong accent came from.

I said I was French by birth, but Australian by choice. One of the very drunken ones shouted: 'F - - - off and return to your country to clean up the mess over there!' (it was the time of the French nuclear tests in the South Pacific). I explained that I was against the nuclear tests, that I had seen the Mediterranean Sea dying, and that I would like to prevent the Pacific Ocean from perishing.

They were very violent and I was close to fighting. I used to do martial arts, so I know how to defend myself when someone comes too close.

I left the group and came back to them with a bucket, trying to fish out the cigarette butts which were floating in the water. This time, I really connected with my love for the dolphins and I asked for protection. I was not in my fight or flight reaction. I was in my dolphin connection, and I felt very protected. I just wanted to stay close to them and to show them another way, someone who cared.

One of the guys said: 'When you are on the sea, you can see so much being dumped in the ocean, that a cigarette butt will not make any difference'.

I replied, 'I personally think that we can all make a difference'.

As we were discussing things in less violent terms, one of the younger guys came up to me and put his cigarette butt in my bucket.

I said, 'If out of our discussion I have touched one person's heart, that's fine. Next time you are at sea, you might not dump anything in the water'. Another guy came to put out his cigarette in my bucket, then a third.

This experience showed me that I was able to get out of the fight or flight reaction into the Dolphin way. When we make eye contact and something happens between us of a higher level than animal fight.

REFERENCES

1 cited in, Amanda Cochrane and Karena Callen, *Dolphins and their Power to Heal.* Bloomsbury, London, 1992.

2 Samuel Sagan, *Awakening the Third Eye.* Clairvision School Press, Sydney, 1990.

3 ibid.

4 ibid.

5 John Lily, *The Centre of the Cyclone,* Bantam Books, New York, 1974.

6 Dr Paul Ameisen, *Every Breath You Take,* Lansdowne Australia, Sydney 1997.

7 James D. Frost, 'Physiological bases of normal EEG rhythms'. In: *Handbook of Electroencephalography and Clinical Neurophysiology.* A Remond, editor. Vol. 6A. Elsevier, Amsterdam, 1976; 150–160.

8 cited in, Michel Odent, *Water and Sexuality.* Penguin/Arkana, New York, 1990.

10

A New Model of Human Potential

Though the search for extra-terrestrial intelligence may take a very long time, we could not do better than to start with a program of rehumanisation by making friends with the whales and the dolphins.

Carl Sagan [1]

Through our research, we are exploring human consciousness, developing different ways to assess human potential, strategies to shift and develop people to their full potential. It became important therefore to develop a model of human psychology which takes account of our results.

A lot of the available psychological instruments measure where people are at, in terms of a traditional view of human consciousness. Very few instruments measure where people *could be* if they were to awaken their full potential, move to a different state of consciousness. It is indeed quite difficult to know how human beings are going to develop in the future.

We have realised that dolphins can lead us into these unknown territories. In their presence, people become fearless, griefless, free of addiction, free of trauma, self-confident, creative, purposeful, unconditional lovers, and connected with spiritual worlds. Is this the direction of human potential? Is this the world to come?

It seems important to have a model which captures our brain research and also the subtle bodies we have described in the last chapter.

If we wanted to link our research to any school of psychology, the Dolphin Within field of study belongs to transpersonal psychology.

TRANSPERSONAL PSYCHOLOGY

The theoretical structure of psychology and psychiatry has been based for a long time on the observations of a rather limited range of mental phenomena and human experiences.

From the time of its establishment in the early 1960s, transpersonal psychology has expanded the field of psychology beyond the psychodynamic/

clinical, behaviourist, cognitive, humanistic and existentialist orientations to include the entire range of human experience.

Abraham Maslow laid the foundations of a new concept of psychology and human nature, based on observations of spontaneously occurring *peak experiences*.[2] In his view, these experiences were supranormal rather than pathological phenomena, and have important implications for the theory of self-actualisation.

Carl Gustav Jung, the founder of analytical psychology, made the most famous and systematic attempt to revise our concepts of the dimensions of human personality. Within his system, the narrow concept of the human unconscious as described by Freud has been considerably expanded to encompass the collective and racial unconscious and a variety of transindividual, primordial and experiential patterns — the archetypes.

Stanislav Grof, studying altered states of consciousness,[3] defined transpersonal experience as 'an expansion or extension of consciousness beyond the usual ego boundaries and the limitations of times and space'.

Transpersonal psychology includes studies of altered states of consciousness, mind—body healing, religious and mystical experience, spiritual growth, teaching and practices, shamanism, meditation, prenatal and perinatal experiences, studies of dying and near–death experiences, as well as the various forms of experiential psychotherapy and psychospiritual transformation.

It is sometimes also called 'fourth force' psychology, centrally concerned with questions of values, meaning, purpose and spirit, while studying human beings in their complex familial, social, ecological, global and cosmic contexts.

Transpersonal psychology has emerged as an independent field of academic study which encompasses and expands upon the 'forces' of psychoanalysis, behaviourism, and humanistic psychology. By looking beyond the individual to a larger view of consciousness, transpersonal psychology creates a point of connection between psychology and spirituality.

A TRANSPERSONAL EXPERIENCE

The Dolphin Within state can be defined as a transpersonal experience. However it is an experience which is not induced by external substances (like drugs), or by someone else (like hypnosis). The Dolphin Within is experienced in a conscious state. It can be viewed as a transpersonal experience of a new type, because it integrates an experience of 'cosmic unity' with an experience of higher self.

> [cosmic unity characteristics are] transcendence of the subject-object dichotomy, exceptionally strong positive effect (peace, tranquillity,

serenity, bliss), a special feeling of sacredness, transcendence of time and space, experience of pure being ('eternity now and infinity here'), and a richness of insights of cosmic relevance. This type of tension-free melted ecstasy can be referred to as 'oceanic ecstasy'.[4]

The Dolphin Within explorers (participants experiencing the Dolphin Within state) are in touch not only with the divine, but with themselves on a higher mode, with their full potential. The Dolphin Within experience is an experience of 'I am' in touch with purpose and full potential.

Our dolphin–human research led us into the *psychophysiology of consciousness*: the study of consciousness associated with different kinds of brainwaves. By using the EEG machine we were able to explore human consciousness and observe three states: an increase of theta, the theta crossover point and the awakened mind.

As we said in the preceding chapter, the Dolphin Within is not only an experience of the etheric body but of the higher self, the divine side of the human nature, with a clear sense of individuality.

The challenge we faced was to develop a model which was not only simple, fun, accurate, attractive and meaningful, but also selected from the animal kingdom some archetypes which could be transferred to the human world at the individual, team and organisational levels.

The dolphin has already been used as a powerful metaphor of leadership in Lynch and Kordis' excellent management book *Strategy of the Dolphin*.[5]

In our consulting work we use a battery of questionnaires to measure values, strategies, brain dominance, team roles and so on. We have added to our assessment strategy the EEG machine, which allows us to give biofeedback on how business people use their brains.

Instead of creating a model based on complex definitions, jargon or codes, we have used our knowledge about the sea and sea creatures to develop a common language across fields of research. In our research, our psychotherapy work, in our individual, group or organisational consulting work, we use the turtle, shark, seahorse and dolphin matrix or the TSSD matrix.

THE TSSD MATRIX *

Our model was developed in conjunction with our friend and colleague Constant Behrens. It looks at a larger view of consciousness and links diverse fields such as psychology and organisational behaviour (marketing).

---

* The *shark–turtle–seahorse–dolphin* matrix is protected under law against any infringement so that only Brand Community Design accredited consultants and partners are entitled to use the model.
© 1996 Brand Community Design, PO Box R1057 Royal Exchange Sydney 2000 Australia

Self expressing   Co-creating

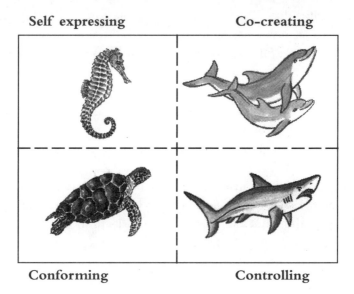

Conforming   Controlling

In this model, and according to Aboriginal legend, we all come out of the *Turtle,* symbol of the mother earth, the prima materia, reflecting a time long past when we were happy blobs, fully in touch with the Divine, but without any sense of self.

Out of this pre-personal stage, we received an ego, and we developed in two basic directions, characterised by the *Shark* (the fighter who wants to survive) or the *Seahorse* (the eccentric who wants to hide and protect his or her individuality). These are the two extremes of the *personal* stage of evolution.

The next stage for human beings is the *transpersonal* stage, where a kind of integration happens between the shark and the seahorse which goes beyond a simple synergy of their respective qualities. It is a transcendental transformation of human qualities, characterised by the *Dolphin*. The transpersonal stage is the transformation from ego to higher self.

EXPERIENCING OUR FULL POTENTIAL

In our perspective, we have all these parts in us, and we all have the dolphin in us as a potential transpersonal experience — that is why we call it the Dolphin Within. The dolphin for us is the archetype of human being, the higher self or the transpersonal stage of humanity: the perfect prototype out of which the seeds of beings originate; and once created, all beings evolve towards the perfection of their archetype.

We do not say that everyone has to be a dolphin, but everyone can experience this transpersonal state, tapping into it and using it. Feeling the

Dolphin Within does not mean repressing the turtle, the shark or the seahorse in us. It means accepting, exploring and transforming them. The key is to explore our full potential, which means exploring all the characters (turtle, shark, seahorse) in us, and be able to reach to the dolphin, which is our higher self.

Using the model of subtle bodies we described earlier, we could say that: the turtle bathes in etheric energy. The seahorse and shark have a lot of astrality (emotions and thoughts). They are the two main characters that we develop through the personal stage of evolution.

The dolphin is our divine side. Once the dolphin is awakened, the turtle, seahorse and shark are no longer characters which pop out whenever, and run the show without our awareness. They are roles the dolphin/self can take if appropriate. Awakening the Dolphin Within means giving awareness and choices in life. It means no longer being a puppet of our turtle, shark or seahorse characters, but starting to be free to create our futures.

Human dolphins do not wonder why they are incarnated on Earth. Dolphins are in touch with their higher selves, they know their purpose and they have a clear vision of what they have come to achieve on Earth, for the benefit of the whole planet rather than for self-interest or self-expression.

The transpersonal dolphin has some commonality with the pre-personal turtle, in terms of spirituality or Divine connection ('cosmic unity'), but brings with it the will of the shark and the heart of the seahorse. The dolphin can be seen as a catalyst for transformation of the planetary consciousness.

The pre-personal turtle will aim at merging with the divine and dissolving all individuality. The personal seahorse and shark have developed a sense of individuality and a certain degree of self-determination, but have lost their unity with the divine. The transpersonal dolphin is a state in which the human higher self is one with the divine, while still retaining individuality.

Viewed from that perspective, the human dolphin doesn't follow the eastern tradition of wanting to escape from earthly incarnations, to become one with the divine. Human dolphins are not meditating on top of mountains and forgetting about the world. They are in the marketplace, making a difference on the planet. Human dolphins want to be on Earth, to combine energy with other Dolphins to achieve their purpose.

The choices we made of turtle, shark, seahorse and dolphin were not arbitrary, as one can see by exploring some of the animals' qualities and extending them into those of their human equivalents. In the course of our work in the business world in particular, we find that people have a strong dominance in one or other of the four quadrants.

TURTLES

Turtles are ancient reptiles; little changed since the time dinosaurs roamed the Earth. Turtles have protective shells into which, when under threat, they withdraw their head, legs and tail.

At no stage in their lives are sea turtles free from predators; as babies they have a low survival rate, and as adults they are prey to sharks and humans. They have no teeth, they swim quite slowly, but if they do survive, they can live longer than most other animals. Sea turtles roam the oceans widely, but they always return to the same beaches to lay their eggs.

Turtles are peaceful. They freeze and retract under danger. Their reptilian brain helps them to go through anything without big reactions or attacks in case of danger.

Human turtles

Human turtles look for stability and security. Physical and emotional comfort is important to them. In return for security and comfort, they give application, obedience, conformity, adherence and compliance. They follow with approval rather than pursue with passion. They also have the capacity for knowing how to truly serve, in the devotional sense.

Human turtles have great powers of concentration, but their attention does not move easily from one topic to another. They are diligent, reliable, patient and dedicated. They pay a lot of attention to details and they are very consistent. They are open and friendly, easy to get on with. They have an air of naivety which can be very engaging. They can be very popular. People like them because they are so easy to approach. They are sympathetic and they know how to listen. Their caring, kindness and modesty make them comfortable to be with. People know they will be heard, and are comforted by the warmth created. Human turtles are diplomatic. They are conscious of how others feel, and they do their best not to hurt others' feelings.

A turtle brain is very low on beta and therefore does not risk being stressed. A turtle brain is also very low in alpha and theta, and therefore does not risk dreaming too much either.

Corporate turtles

I like working with corporate turtles. They tell me everything about the history and tradition of their organisations. For a management consultant, listening to a corporate turtle is very revealing. They know how the company started, the different fortunes or mergers the organisation has been through. They know and care for their people. They act like the organisational archive. Traditional turtles preserve the heritage of a family or an organisation.

Turtle transformation

Turtles lack confidence because they have never challenged themselves, they have never had to get out of their carapace. However, when properly inspired, nurtured and supported, turtles can break through very quickly. They need role models to be inspired, and an 'angel' to encourage them. When turtles go through a Dolphin Within experience, they often laugh to express the feeling of freedom. Once their self-limitations have dissolved, turtles cannot be stopped.

SHARKS

Sharks are anything but primitive; they are very intelligent. They are the most highly adapted fish in the sea. However, their behaviour is basically geared to just two fundamental requirements, feeding and breeding.

Sharks hunt alone, and their lives are entirely controlled by conditioned reflexes. They have a continual, low-intensity feeding drive, but the presence of other sharks introduces an element of competition. The feeding drive is thus exacerbated until the notorious 'feeding frenzy' is generated. Sharks are so voracious that they can readily eat each other.

Sharks are also much maligned; their aggressive behaviour is often exaggerated. Many species of shark are completely harmless, yet they are collectively and universally feared. The film *Jaws* did a lot of damage to shark reputations, painting them as monsters of the deep. White pointer sharks are on the list of endangered species in some countries (including Australia).

Human sharks

A permanent hunger haunts human sharks, and drives their behaviour. Their self-interest, based on the fundamental mechanisms of survival, leads them to a drive for consumption, materialism and competitiveness. Human sharks want to be number one. They need to succeed, and they believe that they can succeed. They like to be in control, to conquer. They have a 'just do it' philosophy. They want action, and they want it now.

Human sharks have no higher purpose; however, they do have goals in life. They have a strong drive to achieve what they want, and the real sharks reach their goals, which are mainly about acquiring material goods. Once achieved, they find other goals. They never stop, always striving for more of the same. There may be a moment of questioning ('What am I running after?'), but they quickly forget about that in the rush to the next material goal.

They communicate through figures. They convert everything into numbers, usually with a dollar sign in front of them. Even their partners are seen as investments! In business, they only focus on the bottom line, nothing else.

Human sharks have strong desires. The shark libido is strong, so they have strong sexual needs. Lovemaking can be like a combat and arguments may arise from this. They often use a point-scoring approach with their partners in life and dealing with them may leave a bitter taste in your mouth. Yet they bring their vitality to a relationship. There is a spark about them; a feeling of ignition, alertness; a liking for intensity and a fire of passion.

Human sharks know how to focus, concentrate and act quickly. They are world-players and great achievers. However, because beta is their dominant brainwave frequency, rather than alpha or theta, they never slow down their brains and they end up over-stressed and burnt out. Because of this, they find it difficult to relax and often need to drink, smoke or take drugs to do so. This produces side effects such as lack of clarity. In order to combat this, they also use coffee, tea and other stimulants to keep them going. They are thus trapped in a vicious circle of relaxants and stimulants.

Human sharks are drawn to people with dynamism. They have little tolerance for dreamers whose hopes and wishes never amount to anything. They are not inspired by weak philosophers or intellectuals. They are not drawn to the helpless or destitute, but rather look up to successful people. They are daring people who like to use their muscle power.

Human sharks are successful achievers, in business, sport and military careers. They can have an angry character which creates barriers between them and others, making it hard for people to reach them.

Corporate sharks

I swim with dolphins in the ocean, but I meet sharks on land, especially in the business world. When I was doing my MBA, the business school was training us to become the biggest sharks in the pool. My ex-husband and my ex-boss were both sharks. I apply the same strategy to human sharks as I do with sharks in the sea: I face them without fear.

I respect and value corporate sharks for their actions, focus and results; because they get what they want and they want big. They have their own self-discipline. They create waves of initiative or movement, and are good at getting other people to move, since they provide the impetus. They have a lot of stamina and are great achievers with the capacity to do things which other people only think about doing. They take the initiative, without hesitation. If there's a measure to take, they take it, without procrastination.

I feel compassion for corporate sharks because they are paying a high price (health, family, friends) for their high drive.

Shark transformation

Human sharks are very resistant to dolphin talk. They are often cynical, sceptical, or even aggressive. By taking them out of their usual environment to sail, snorkel, connect with dolphins, and scuba dive, they are no longer in control; their armour cracks and their Dolphin Within appears. When they go through a Dolphin Within experience, human sharks often cry, they release the tension and the pain they have spent their life hiding.

SEAHORSES

The seahorse is a fish, but a pretty unorthodox one. It has the head of a horse, the tail of a monkey, and it swims in an upright position. Even more interesting, the seahorse has a kangaroo-like pouch, and it is the male seahorse which carries the one hundred eggs! The male contorts his body and expels the young, miniature adults, through a single opening. Seahorses mate for life — they know the meaning of commitment!

When divers first find seahorses underwater, hiding in seagrass, their usual reaction is one of amazement and wonder at such a strangely beautiful and delicate creature. In Australia there is a unique seahorse called the *leafy sea dragon*, which takes the 'normal' seahorse qualities much further and is truly mind-boggling.

Human seahorses

Human seahorses have a deep need to express themselves, to preserve their individuality, to stand out, to differentiate themselves from the norm to the extent of appearing eccentric. They have the capacity to receive higher inspiration. Thus they are often creative, and they like to play with myths and legends. They create their own world in order to live their own fantasies. They have a strong sense of show. They like to surprise, to amaze, to inspire awe and wonder.

They are very creative and unorthodox. They take care of their physical appearance. Their hair styles, clothes, accessories and cars are often used as ways to express their individuality and oddity.

They have charm and, often, physical appeal that draws others to them. They like to spend time pursuing cultural interests. They pay frequent visits to art galleries and museums. They can spend hours in the art gallery, just enjoying the aesthetics of the place. They have an artistic disposition. All forms of the arts interest them. They resonate easily with others involved in creative activity.

Human seahorses have many admirers, and lots of relationships. They have a very sensual and romantic nature. They have a way of seducing through the sheer power of attraction.

Human seahorses have access to alpha and theta brainwaves which put them into a creative mode. However, they are often not shifting their brain as an act of choice, but suddenly find themselves off the planet, up in the clouds.

Corporate seahorses

There are few corporate seahorses in organisations. They have difficulties surviving because they are so different. They are known for their eccentricity and they are not team players. They differentiate themselves in their values, thinking and behaviours from any norms. They have difficulties fitting into teams. They are attractive and bring diversity to an organisation. They are very precious and often undervalued.

I like working with corporate seahorses because of their creative, lateral thinking and inventiveness. They have the courage to stand out and to be different, even if it is often at a very high cost.

Seahorse transformation

Seahorses have a very high opinion of themselves which covers deeply held self-doubts fostered through the difficulties they have to face in order to survive. Seahorses going through a Dolphin Within experience often become very quiet. Instead of using the air time to express themselves, seahorses realise that they can 'be' without have to defend their right for difference, individuality. They slowly find a place of peace instead, and want to be part of the pod. Through the program, they learn to value their theta state (creativity) and to understand and access more of their beta (focus) brainwave.

DOLPHINS

It is said that dolphins evolved from land mammals which went back to the sea about 25–50 million years ago. Living in the supportive marine environment, they had access to three-quarters of the surface of the planet, and they experienced no gravity. In this environment they evolved a very advanced brain.

Dolphins' brains have access to alpha and theta brainwaves, as John Lilly's research has shown.

> I suspect that whales and dolphins quite naturally go in the directions we
> call spiritual, in that they get into meditative states quite simply and easily.

Dolphins breathe consciously; they do not sleep, because if they lose consciousness, they drown. It has been shown that, to rest, they shut down one side of their brain at a time in a kind of meditation.

They have a very highly developed sound sense; they can hear the sound of a whistle as much as twenty kilometres away. They can pick up each other's signals over ten kilometres. With their sonar system they can differentiate shapes and sizes which are indistinguishable to the human eye. They send a stream of high frequency 'clicks' — focused sound in a narrow beam — projected from the forehead. This blast of ultrasonic vibration hits an object, and the returning signal is analysed by the dolphin to give it a three-dimensional, holographic picture; thus they can 'see' right inside us. Dolphins can locate two different targets simultaneously, whilst at the same time communicating with each other through whistling. They can kill or stun their prey by blasting them with high-energy 'clicks', it has been shown that they can emit a focused beam of sound carrying two kilowatts of energy.

Dolphins are thought to pass information to one another in the form of pictograms. If they detect the presence of a shark, they don't need to send a verbal alarm, because the echo is picked up by other dolphins; the information is shared (like a torch in the darkness — one person has it, but everyone can see what it lights up). What is more, each dolphin has its own whistle 'signature', like a name.

> If a human diver jumps into the water with a dolphin, the dolphin can 'see'
> inside the diver into the air passages of his lungs and respiratory system.
> This is because sonar sight penetrates materials that are approximately the
> same density as the water — like human flesh — and returns different
> echoes from objects with different densities [...] To the dolphin, the
> diver might look like an x-ray photograph of the human body.[6]

Dolphins live in elaborate, sophisticated societies, numbering from a few to a hundred or more. They are the only mammals, apart from humans, that make love for fun and not only for reproduction. They make love belly-to-belly like humans, too! It is said that they spend one-third of their time feeding, one-third meditating and one-third making love.

> In courtship and lovemaking, for example, dolphins emphasise the difference
> between everyday life and the courting by changing the body posture. In
> everyday life, the body is relatively straight and horizontal; in courtship, the
> dolphin bends his body at all points possible, forming an S-shaped curve, a
> strong signal of something special happening.[7]

Human dolphins

Human dolphins can self-regulate their brains. They can have full access to their left (logical) brains and their right (intuitive) brains, and they can integrate the two. They know how to produce at will beta (for action), alpha (for relaxation) or theta (for creativity) and delta (for healing) brainwaves. They do consciously what most people do unconsciously and automatically. They therefore have more choices in life. They spend a lot of time in the meditative state characterised by theta brainwaves, for creative inspiration and peak health. They do not sleep a lot; they meditate.

Because human dolphins can slow down their brains as an act of will, they do not need to smoke or drink alcohol to relax. On the other hand, because they can also speed up their brains, they do not need coffee, tea or other stimulants. They have no addictions, nor dependency on anything or anybody.

Through their brain play, human dolphins have a clear vision of their full potential and of a process of self-transformation which will lead them to incarnate their higher selves. They explore and face any parts of themselves and transform them. As visionary leaders, their vision becomes reality.

Because human dolphins know what their higher selves want, they are unstoppable. They are able to accomplish things which are commonly seen as impossible; they can move mountains. They can tap into their full energy power and survive anything. They have their own self-discipline, they do not need outside incentives or motivations to achieve their purpose in life.

Human dolphins show confidence and purposefulness. People do not question them, because they sense their 'knowingness' and their truth. There is a joy that springs from inside, not from external events nor as a reaction to someone else. They radiate vitality. They have a capacity for certitude, and for knowingness. They are uplifting, and can be inspiring to others. Because they acknowledge the shark, turtle and seahorse sides of themselves, human dolphins accept, understand, value and respect the shark, turtle and seahorse characters of others. They give unconditional love: love without trade. They are non-judgmental; they accept people just the way they are. They have deep feelings, not reactive emotions. They are free from co-dependent attachment. They access their free will and choice, and they provide a space where their partners, friends and work colleagues can exercise their freedom and choices as well.

Human dolphins do not use their reptilian brains in a 'fight or flight' survival response; they bypass the reptilian brain and use their neo-cortex. Instead of reacting, they play.

They have a highly developed sixth sense: their 'sonar system'. They use it to scan people and 'tune in' to their emotions and their state of consciousness. For example, they intuitively know when people tell the truth and when they are lying, and they always tell the truth themselves. They communicate through telepathy like the Aborigines.

Human dolphins can see their own full potential, or higher self. They have techniques to explore different states of consciousness, to unlock memories, to bypass time constraints and use their vision to travel into the past and the future. However, they are not caught up in a purely self-exploration journey nor are they trying to reprogram themselves through creative visualisation techniques. Their approach is to experience deep states of consciousness.

Human dolphins prefer the truth to a rose-coloured story. They are not lost in the past or the future; they live in the here and now. They care for the environment, the earth and the ocean, and they do more with less; they don't waste time, energy or space. They don't waste time on problems, they focus on creative solutions and their implementation. They act accordingly through small and practical actions which make a difference. They minimise their waste, they recycle. They clean beaches, the countryside and the oceans.

Human dolphins spend a lot of time with nature, in particular by, on and in the sea. They love swimming, snorkelling and scuba diving. They have a vegetarian diet, motivated by a care for animals and for the health benefits. They don't eat fish or seafood, because they spend a lot of time underwater playing with them. However they do eat seaweed, which provides Omega 6 fatty acid — the brain food.

Truth is important to them, as are results and outcomes. Fiercely loyal, they stand by their partners through thick and thin. When they make love, it is a spiritual experience for them and their partners.

Their 'pod' extends beyond their immediate family. They make friends for life. They have responsibility, courage and purity of heart. They are calm, confident and self-centred, in the spiritual sense. They like to have fun. They have a strong vitality that their partners can benefit from too.

They give unconditional love which is based on high involvement and high detachment. They do not create relationships based on the A-frame or co-dependent model, where the two branches collapsed if separated. They create H-frame relationships where the two people grow strongly and connect to each other, not because of need but to co-create.

High involvement	High involvement/detachment
Seahorse	Dolphin
Turtle	Shark

Low detachment	High detachment

They enjoy change and learning; they direct their own change, and learn by playing. They are change catalysts for themselves, others and the planet.

Self-expression	Self-transformation
Seahorse	*Dolphin*
Turtle	*Shark*

Self-giving   **Self-driving**

Human dolphins connect different fields like research, education, business and environmental protection, and create their own professions. They are catalysts, role models; they create breakthroughs. They are continuously learning, researching, sharing and bringing change on the planet. Human Dolphins also use the latest technology, in terms of computers and telecommunication. They love the Internet, presenting as it does the opportunity to make global connections between people and to share information and knowledge freely.

Corporate dolphins

Corporate dolphins are very rare and precious assets in an organisation: they are visionary and futuristic. They can foresee the changes in the business environment and help organisations to anticipate these changes and be ready for them. They generate energy to bring the vision of the organisation beyond the bottom line which will get all stakeholders inspired to work in a cooperative way, to co-create in order to bring the organisation's shared vision into reality.

Human dolphins do not work, they play — or rather they have no boundaries between work and play. Their work is a playground for their vision to become reality. Whatever they do is fulfilling their purpose. They live in the high fulfilment, high achievement quadrant.

High fulfilment	High purpose
Seahorse	*Dolphin*
Turtle	*Shark*

Low achievement   **High achievement**

They inspire others and work in a cooperative way to bring their vision to reality. Human dolphins work and play well, both individually and in pods. They are sincere — people can feel they are genuine. Their magnanimity, dignity and noble nature are glowing magnets to which others are drawn. They make strong friendships, founded on qualities such as trust, respect and sincerity. Others like to bask in their warmth and enthusiasm. They foster connections between people. They do not compete but work cooperatively to achieve their shared vision.

Community builders

Extending the learning from the dolphins and from the humans to humanity, we could say that the purpose of humanity may be to build communities linked together for a higher purpose, the same way dolphins are able to live in very highly developed communities. Through the Dolphin Society, we are building a community of dolphin carers.

The TSSD matrix provides a blueprint for understanding individual make-up which can be applied equally as well to a team, to a whole organisation and indeed to any community.

An organisation is really a group of diverse stakeholders linked by a certain common interest (a stake): management, employees, customers, shareholders, interest groups, government, strategic partners, competitors.

Once the members of an organisation understand their turtle, seahorse and shark sides, once they get in touch with their full potential, they can start working together. By sharing a dream, vision and core values based on their full potential (not on their limiting characters), they start building a community around an organisation. We facilitate the discovery of the Dolphin Within of different stakeholders of an organisation.

Bringing the Dolphins into the business world means that we are no longer management consultants but *community builders,* swimming in the world of environment and social ecology.

REFERENCES

1 Carl Sagan, *The Cosmic Connection,* Doubleday, USA, 1973.

2 Abraham Maslow, *Religions, Values, and Peak Experiences,* Viking, New York, 1970.

3 Stanislav Grof, 'Variety of Transpersonal experiences: observations from LSD psychotherapy', In: Stanley R Dean, *Psychiatry and Mysticism,* Nelson-Hall, Chicago, 1975; 311.

4 Dudley Lynch and Paul Kordis, *Strategy of the Dolphin,* Fawcett-Columbine, New York, 1988.

5 ibid.

6 Peter Warshall, 'The Ways of the Whales' in *Mind in the Water,* Joan MacIntyre (ed.), Sierra Book Club, San Francisco, 1974.

7 ibid.

11

DOLPHINS INTO THE BUSINESS WORLD

ODB CONSULTING'S MISSION

We created ODB Consulting to bring the dolphins' message into the business world. Our mission is *to awaken individuals, teams and organisations to their full potential*. Through our research, we have designed a method for the business world, including a full set of assessment tools which allow us to assess and develop the values, behaviours and performance of an individual, a team and an organisation.

THE DELPHI PROCESS

When applied to an individual, our method uses self-assessment questionnaires as well as observers' assessment questionnaires. In this way we get a person's view of themselves and the views of others who live and work with them, which provides a great depth of understanding of their full potential.

Our method, the Delphi Process, is more than just a battery of instruments and tests. It is a complete process and philosophy which allows participants, be they individuals or teams, to see their current reality clearly and to have a shared understanding of it.

Individual Full Potential

	Not known to Self	Known to Self
Known to Others	BLIND	OPEN
Not known To Others	UNKNOWN	HIDDEN

Adapted from the Johari window

We do more than just assess and write reports on an individual or a team. We facilitate processes in which individuals and teams get a direct experience of their full potential. Our interactive processes facilitate exploring and discovering more about themselves, more about their characters: their *open, hidden, blind* and *unknown.* We use experiential learning techniques wherever possible, and we also have an emphasis on activities related to the ocean, to the dolphins' world, which we access through sailing, snorkelling, scuba diving and many other water activities.

The aim of our method is to give individuals a tangible experience and a clear understanding of their turtle side (their heritage), their shark side (their power), their seahorse side (their uniqueness) and their dolphin side (their higher purpose). The Delphi Process is aimed at finding out more about the *hidden, blind* and *unknown* parts of individuals, to give a clear picture of their full potential and a strategic action plan to realise their potential. This process creates a 'creative tension'★ within individuals, giving them an experience of their full potential, and a strategy, a knowledge of how to use it, how to bring their vision into reality in their professional and private lives.

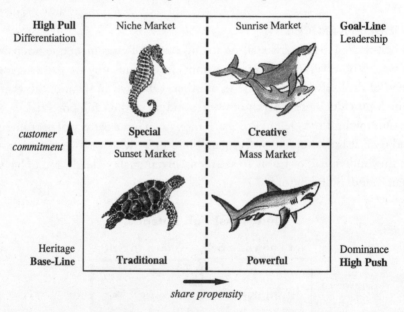

The uniqueness of this approach is that it can be applied to individuals, to a team, and to a whole organisation through the process of creating a vision, a mission and the identification of a critical set of core competencies to assess and develop within the organisation.

★ Peter M Singe, *The Fifth Disciplines.* Century Business, UK, 1992.

AWAKENING ORGANISATIONS TO THEIR FULL POTENTIAL

An organisation is a living organism providing products and services to another living organism, its customers. Both organisms are a combination of complex parameters such as age, colour, gender, physical characteristics, sexual orientation, educational background, ethnicity, family background, language, family responsibilities, level or function, lifestyle, marital status, political beliefs, religion, skills, socioeconomic status, thinking patterns, work background, values — the list is almost endless.

In traditional human resources work, a human resource manager and/or consultant assesses the people according to the company's current needs or current culture, and rejects the ones that don't fit. In traditional marketing work, a marketing manager and/or consultant segments the market and focuses on delivering products or services to suit current users' needs, to get the largest market shares. Usually, market research will not consult non-users of the products or services, or eccentric users. In organisations, managers or employees who challenge the status quo and differentiate themselves are usually 'let go'.

The Delphi Process does not focus on selecting segments and a specific profile of managers, we embrace the overall diversity of the spectrum. We look at all stakeholders — shareholders, management, employees, customers, competitors, interest groups, government bodies — as one community with different value systems. The aim is to discover more about the *blind, hidden* and *unknown* parts of an organisation in order to discover more about its *full potential*.

We collect the maximum of information on the organisation, listening to all the different stakeholders (through focus groups, surveys, interviews, etc). We want to know what they have to say about the products or service the organisation is delivering in order to assess the potential of the product or service the organisation could deliver.

While collecting information we also assess all stakeholders giving us the information, especially their values and their worldview, on our TSSD matrix. The turtles (the belongers), the sharks (the achievers), seahorses (the differentiators), the dolphins (the prophets). The TSSD matrix allows us to find out more about the open, hidden, blind and unknown qualities of the community. Using the TSSD matrix above allows us to structure the information given as follows:*

---

* Constant Behrens's application of the model to marketing.

TSSD ORGANISATIONAL MATRIX	
THE DIFFERENTIATOR SEAHORSES Differentiators tell you what attracts customers to the organisation. How the organisation can differentiate itself from others in the field. A different, surprising new approach to the business, market, services, etc.	**THE PROPHET DOLPHINS** Prophets tell you what they foresee about where the world is going tomorrow. How the organisation can get ready for the coming changes. A futuristic, visionary approach to the business, market, services, etc.
THE BELONGER TURTLES Belongers tell you what they like about the organisation today. How the organisation came into being, its heritage, values, behaviours. A tried and true approach to maintaining the business, market, services, etc.	**THE ACHIEVER SHARKS** Achievers tell you how the organisation is successful today. How the organisation can grow and prosper in today's reality. A market share-driven approach to the business, market, services, etc.

FACILITATING COMMUNITY CHANGE

Measuring, understanding, valuing and managing the diversity and complexity of an organisation, when seen as a whole community, as an asset rather than a liability, means anticipating and facilitating the change process with a large number of variables. Once the variables are in the TSSD window, the full potential of an organisation is revealed. It becomes the blueprint for a change strategy, where dolphins define the higher purpose and competitive advantage of the organisation; sharks translate the purpose into practical actions; seahorses provide a pool of ideas which differentiates the organisation; and turtles nurture the organisation and preserve a sense of heritage and place.

The process is constant and interactive. The community shapes the organisation by being consulted and listened to, and the organisation also shapes the community by listening to the seahorses' eccentricity and the dolphins' futuristic visions, rather than only considering the shark or turtle viewpoints. By unlocking its full potential, an organisation can become the voice of an entire global community.

DISCOVERING THE SHARK AND TURTLE

We use drawing in our focus group sessions, as a way of capturing information which is sometimes difficult to formulate through words (which requires the logical and rational intervention of the left brain more than the creativity of the right brain). Through a drawing, individuals communicate feelings and thoughts which are often still not fully formulated in their consciousness.

Critical information is collected through a picture created by an individual or a team; the seahorse part, the shark part, or the full potential dolphin part. When individuals and teams present their drawings, they tell us in an evocative but usually non-threatening language the different traumas, pains and successes they have been through. The drawings help to process or heal the hurts; in front of their bosses, they are able to tell me the truth.

One of our large clients' manager focus groups came up with the following to describe the turtle and shark sides:

Turtle side: My organisation is like a dinosaur because it has trouble adapting to a changing environment.

Shark side: If you do not conform you will get the axe.

One of our projects was to write a business plan for an organisation which was to become the quality 'shepherd' of an entire industry. We assessed the experts' view of their industry by running focus groups and surveys. The focus group was designed and structured around the *Roadrunner* cartoon, which is a powerful way to create a fun atmosphere to relax and unlock the participants' brains so that they are less inhibited about telling the truth.

The industry experts came up with the following drawings which they presented to the whole group.

My industry is like...

A centipede: many legs take me in many directions down many paths.

A game of pass the parcel: everyone tries to pass responsibilities for quality on to the other parties.

A prostitute: happy to take the money and get into bed with anyone, without any responsibility.

This information, combined with surveys and statistical analysis, gave us a clear understanding of the current reality; the shark side, or the hidden nature of the industry.

DISCOVERING THE DOLPHIN PART OF A TEAM

In our team-building or 'dolphin-podding' programs, we ask participants to make drawings depicting their organisation, using metaphors like that of a sea-going vessel.

In one project with a large cosmetic and pharmaceutical organisation, we did a team-building program for sixty of their people, including their managing director, a woman who had just been promoted. The brief for their drawing exercise was as follows:

> Imagine that you have been through a long ocean journey, and that your division is an ocean-going vessel going through different weather conditions. You are now in the dry dock, building a new vessel for the future. What are the two pictures you see — the vessel of the past, and the vessel of the future?

Through the metaphor of the vessel, the nine teams expressed and shared the common reality about the organisation's past, their shark side, in an indirect and safe way; depicting storms, sharks, cannons and fire.

They also expressed enthusiasm, optimism, goodwill, creativity and

commitment towards the future; their dolphin side, with modern vessels which welcomed the new managing director and her family, while the ex-MD was disappearing into the water. They depicted their future with sun, direction, trust, teamwork and dolphins.

Through such processes, the past and its difficulties are processed, the learning is capitalised, and a shared vision of the future emerges for the whole organisation.

EXPERIENCING THE OCEAN

A central part of our consulting approach is to bring business people to the ocean. The best way to become corporate dolphins, dolphin pods and dolphin organisations is to go sailing, swimming or scuba diving together. Most of our programs have an outdoor activity component which involves an oceanic adventure. We integrate a Cousteau-type expedition into our methods.

While we can run our outdoor programs from anywhere by the sea, using houseboats, sailing boats, canoes etc., the place we like to go to best is Port Stephens, where we run the Dolphin Within research and therapy programs, because the dolphins live there and corporate people can have a Dolphin Within experience. This is the quickest and best change process we can imagine.

The Anchorage, a fantastic marina and conference centre, is our

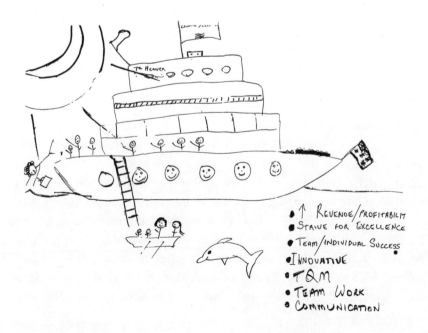

157

management school. We see it as the university of the future, combining accommodation, conference room, restaurants and a fleet of yachts and boats. The area has islands with hut and tent accommodation, and the dolphins as teachers! Instead of being in a dark conference room, our participants are on the water, learning by doing, learning how to face the constant changes in their environment; wind, rain, sun, moon, tide etc., learning how to work together to put sails up, tack, jibe, finding the direction they want to go, and discovering how to use their resources efficiently.

Our method is aimed at developing corporate dolphins free of fear, anger or pain, encouraging them to share deeply their lives, their emotions and their feelings, to develop trust and partnership. We facilitate their switching into a new brainwave pattern, involving more alpha and theta, exploring their creativity and their full potential.

Throughout our programs, participants can monitor their brainwaves and assess their own performance, see when they enter a theta state and learn how to access that state. They become aware of the way they use their brains, experience a theta state and even a delta state, learn to regulate their brainwave activity and become able to enter a desired state of consciousness at will.

WHEN BANKERS MEET THE DOLPHINS

On the second anniversary of my motorbike accident, we were running our first corporate dolphin workshop for a group of bankers. Dolphinicity again.

The conference was about risk-taking for a group of people in a particular division of the bank. John was the manager of the division. At our first meeting, he mentioned that he was going to bring his boat to The Anchorage for the conference. We got along straight away through our common passion for the sea. We told him that he might see some dolphins on the way. He was also worried about the weather, so we mentioned that we had put in an order for sun and a nice breeze!

When we saw him on the Friday night at The Anchorage, the first thing he told us was that he had seen some dolphins near Pittwater! His eyes were shining and I could see his joy, even if he could not express it fully; his bankish culture prevented him from opening his heart like a kid — as yet.

At that stage, the weather was not as promised, but on Saturday morning the sky was blue and the wind had dropped considerably. At two o'clock, when we started our adventure, the wind picked up beautifully as we started sailing. It dropped again when we anchored and started swimming and snorkelling, and picked up again when we needed to sail back to the Anchorage.

After a good meditation, William and I started the group briefing in the conference room, and we described our dolphin model. The presentation was very informal, with laminated flip charts we had created.

William was very aware of being able to ask for and get the necessary elements for running a perfect workshop. He even mentioned to Frank, the skipper of the boat we were using, that everything would be perfect, but that something unexpected would happen and then the dolphins would come.

The unexpected certainly happened. As we went out of the bay on board the big catamaran *Imagine*, someone saw a fin. I looked at it, knowing that it wasn't a dolphin's fin but a shark's. The creature did not breathe and dive as usual, but drifted along in a straight line. I had a moment of concern, thinking the bankers might be terrified and refuse to snorkel. I thought that we really needed to see dolphins next. As we went back into the bay, I asked William to take out his guitar.

The key for our intervention was to create a dolphin experience which they would always remember. I will always remember the 24 banking analysts crowding at the front of the catamaran, watching the dolphins coming and saying hello while William was playing music and singing to them!

At that point, everyone wanted to jump in. I quickly organised the snorkelling activity, showing them the dolphin swim. The dolphins were not far away and I could still hear them when I went in. We can't say that they were swimming with dolphins, but it was important that after seeing the shark they got rid of their fears and were able to jump in — to take a risk. We then anchored in a cove and went snorkelling with the fish, feeding them.

The whole workshop was about experiencing the dolphins' way of being, and translating that into doing business. We had our debriefing on board the boat on the way back to the marina. The bankers did beautiful drawings of their experience and we ran a brain research information session and a brainstorming session on the qualities of a dolphin.

Most of the people were in alpha and theta stage by that time. William closed off the session by singing a song and we had a group photo on the deck.

We ended up that night in Fame Cove, William and myself, in a state of bliss.

In a follow-up conversation with John, he said how happy he was with the workshop and also that on his way back to Sydney on Sunday afternoon, he was passing a beach close to Newcastle and a hundred dolphins came to see him. He also said that he and his family would be interested in coming with us one day to see the whales. He has the connection now. We created corporate dolphins in a bank!

A TURTLE ORGANISATION FINDS ITS DOLPHIN SIDE

One of our projects was a strategic planning program for a small company that provides information about telecommunications and information technology.

Strategic planning is firstly about establishing where you want to go, and secondly working backwards to plan the implementation. We designed an adventure which reflects the same process. The team of seven arrived for a two-day playshop aboard a houseboat. Their first task was to find out where to go, and how to get there together, working as a pod.

Once they found the dolphin bay sanctuary and achieved the first tasks, they reflected on their performance and learned how to work together better. They could see how each member of the team played a critical role, and they built up trust between each other. We videotaped all their activities, so that they could review and reflect on their individual and team performance.

The next phase was to transpose the process to the organisation itself; where do we want to go together?

Living on a houseboat, cooking together, swimming and floating together, all of the team were more relaxed; their brains were producing more alpha. In this relaxing atmosphere, the team was empowered to run the sessions themselves, and the managing director became very inspired when he saw the higher purpose of the organisation in a clear picture of its full potential, which gave meaning to the current situation.

During the first morning session he suddenly stood up as he saw that the organisation's purpose was to give to key decision-makers timely information on technology, which would help them to catch the new waves of change. The group then realised the importance of their role within their industry. They slowly started to see what the managing director was seeing, started to share his vision of their common purpose.

Just at that moment, William said, 'I have important news to share with you; there are dolphins around the boat!'

We were anchored in the dolphin sanctuary where we usually sleep at night, and the dolphins had just joined us! This was true dolphinicity, happening just when the group was getting in touch with their corporate Dolphin Within.

Once their shared purpose was clear, it was relatively easy to write a strategic plan to bring the vision into reality. They were very creative in finding ways to obtain the information through a global network, analyse it, add value with their knowledge and integrity, and distribute it using the technology of tomorrow; the Internet, video and other channels.

DOLPHINS, OUR CORPORATE FACILITATORS

We ran a dolphin podding program for a famous financial information provider, including their managing director. We went canoeing the first day and sailing the second day, using three yachts. The whole pod got together for lunch on a beautiful beach. As the team was eating, I suddenly realised that the managing director was at the centre of a circle formed by all his people. He was offering them strawberries from a plate, a gesture full of softness, a very dolphin-like behaviour which was very different from his usual shark-like habits.

At that particular instant, someone shouted, 'Dolphins!'

The dolphins appeared right in front of the beach, jumping out of water! Another moment of dolphinicity! It is interesting to notice that, whilst being with dolphins helps people discover their Dolphin Within, when the people act as dolphins themselves the dolphins often join in.

I felt really supported by them, they were part of my consulting team, running the dolphin podding program with me, appearing at the critical moment to remind everyone what it means to be a corporate dolphin.

These experiences illustrate how unique the programs we run can be, in terms of supporting participants to find and explore their Dolphin Within. At work, they are used to being turtles or sharks. By providing an environment safe enough to let the dolphin side (full potential, unknown) appear, individuals and teams start new patterns of relationship.

DEVELOPING A POD OF SEVENTY DOLPHINS

As we were designing and organising another dolphin podding program, for a large car manufacturer, David the training manager joined us at The Anchorage for a day, coming from Melbourne to meet us and see the place. The event involved 70 male master technicians, the cream of the organisation in terms of problem solving and customer service. We met David at the airport in our dolphin minibus, and took him to The Anchorage for lunch.

The objective of the event was team building and reward for an excellent year of work. David was a charming person, very concerned for his people and obviously used to working hard to check every detail. He was concerned that something could go wrong in planning a two-day workshop for 70 men using oceanic adventures. It's true that it involved a lot of logistics on our side. David wanted a 'Plan B' in case of bad weather. William had difficulties explaining to him that we organised the weather as well!

That day of our meeting, the weather was beautiful, and David said as we were walking around visiting the conference rooms, 'It's really a day for sailing'.

I said, 'Let's go, then!'

I knew that the best way to show him what we were doing was to go sailing instead of having a traditional meeting in a room, so we took *Sirius*, I dropped my business blue dress and high heels for swimmers and a T-shirt, and William gave David the wheel. He was like a little kid discovering a new toy; his face changed and he just opened totally. Back at The Anchorage, he was much more relaxed about the whole event.

We knew that it would be great, and it happened to be a fantastic event. All 70 guys worked beautifully together. We had a huge fleet of yachts, and the big catamaran as a mother ship. They all had to find their destination (shared vision), learn to sail through a quick training from the skipper on board, and be totally in charge of their yachts for the whole day. They found the dolphin sanctuary and managed to go ashore to pick up needed information there. They swapped boats to return to The Anchorage on time, in peace. They managed to spot dolphins, to achieve all their team assessment questionnaires and problem-solving activities which were part of the voyage.

The day after, David had to leave for Europe for a meeting at the organisation's headquarters. I got the 70 men into a huge circle around him and gave him a huge dolphin card signed by everyone, thanking him for organising the program. As a training manager, he was used to giving and nurturing his people; it was the first time he had received such a touching thanks. They wished him good luck in joining the sharks in Europe!

After David's departure, we all boarded one large boat to go and discover the dolphins. We saw a pod which stayed with us; two dolphins did a synchronised jump as we approached! There was a net rigged out from the side of the boat, which the braver participants could go into to see the dolphins underwater; I was in the net with about twenty men, with the dolphins swimming all around us.

After that experience, the group went snorkelling and fed the fish, and had lunch on board. During lunch one of them said to me: 'Olivia, I have never experienced such a state, where I just stop like that'.

'Yes, beingness instead of doingness,' I replied. 'It's a valuable state for accessing creativity, reducing stress and having insights about yourself. The sea's the quickest way to reach this state. Do you have a favourite activity which gives you this feeling?'

'Yes, I love cycling,' he said.

'So, it's important to take the time to do it,' I suggested.

'But I always have something to do, even at home, my wife asks me to cut the grass!'

'You'll have to explain to her that it's your strategic time. You need it to get into a peak performance state. It's the time when your brain slows down and you recharge.'

We ended the program with some strategic action plans to integrate their learning to the office and their private life.

Just after lunch, as we were going to leave the bay, a pod of dolphins came past the boat; I jumped in. I swam my dolphin swim and I was swimming with happiness and joy underwater when three dolphins came and swam just under me, making eye contact with me. It was a beautiful gift after two days of corporate training!

FROM AN OIL COMPANY TO A NEW ENERGY COMPANY

Working with our friend and colleague, Constant Behrens, with an oil company, we were called in to facilitate a vision-setting workshop in which the company's top team had to decide about the future of the organisation. How could we transform an oil company into a dolphin company?

Through our method, the top team identified the company's turtle culture, but with a touch of shark teeth. They provided such phrases as 'oil company complex', 'profit driven', 'non-controversial', 'quietly competent', 'modest', 'analysis driven', 'solid', 'safe' and 'enduring'.

Following the benchmarking of their own company and their competitors, the participants committed themselves to creating a dolphin organisation. They identified their mission as being to solve the world's energy problem, to provide energy solutions for the future, energising the world and energising their customers.

They created the new organisation's core values; passion, energy, growth and spirit.

They positioned themselves as a dolphin company, as the first oil company to break free, looking at total energy needs, at an effective use of scarce resources, promoting energy efficiency. An organisation that delivers tangible products and services which save time and energy.

We knew that success for an oil company would depend on re-defining the future of the industry as a whole, rather than settling for the status quo; rethinking the concept of *Energy, Efficiency* and *Environment* beyond commodity fuels. This means exploring new sources of energy and looking at other ways to save the environment.

We created a process where the top team itself discovered this, and then committed themselves to implement the change.

WHEN SHARKS TRY TO IMITATE DOLPHINS

I was really surprised when, early in September 1996, I got a call from a friend who worked in the Sydney office of one of the world's biggest and most prestigious management consulting companies.

He told me: 'Olivia, we're working for an Australian retail bank, and we're looking for a creative workshop which will help us to see a completely different view of the retail banking service. We think that being with dolphins might help us'.

Anyone who knows the company my friend worked for would also know that wanting to be with dolphins to be more creative was a big paradigm shift in their approach; you can understand my surprise.

By working closely with them and their client during September and October, we were getting ready for the November workshop. At the last minute we got a call telling us that they no longer needed our services. We later found out that they were going ahead with the workshop we had designed for them, but they intended to run it themselves.

The thought of one of the world's most powerful consulting companies trying to imitate ODB Consulting is quite interesting. My only concern was that they were using only a shell of what we do, without taking the research on brain technology and the philosophy of our approach. They were acting like sharks imitating dolphins.

I called a meeting with one of the managing directors of the consulting company. At the meeting I named the shark game they were playing, and I asked him if the organisation wanted to go on playing the game. In response he said, 'We aren't aware of playing a shark game'.

The shark strategy is the norm in business, because 'it's a shark-eat-shark world out there'. They weren't even aware of the unprofessional way they behaved, because it was the norm for them.

The managing director liked my metaphor, and he promised to look into the issue. A few days later, he told me on the phone that they had tried before to run a workshop with external consultants, and it didn't work. Apparently their own people took over and ran the workshop (a shark strategy), while the external consultant sat for two days with nothing to do. The client didn't find this extra cost justifiable.

Frightened to reproduce the same mistake, instead of learning from it and ensuring that it wouldn't happen again, they had decided to run the show without any external consultant. They took over at the design phase, using our ideas but not our services.

I tried without success to show them the game and the pattern they were trapped in, at the expense of their client. They didn't want to recognise any game. However, they agreed to pay us some fees for the time we put into designing the workshop.

They had their workshop at The Anchorage, just as we had designed it. They had a boat trip to see the dolphins, but as my friend described it to me afterwards, 'It rained for two days and the boat trip was terrible. I felt as if we were being punished!'

I'm not sure their client is going to revolutionise the retail banking industry when the consultants they employ are themselves so cautious, avoiding getting out of their comfort zone!

CORPORATE DOLPHIN CONSULTANTS

I recently attended an alumni reunion of the MBA students with whom I graduated five years earlier. I was very interested to see what their lives were like.

Most were corporate turtles, working in the public sector, complaining about the slowness of the system but not doing anything about it, nor leaving it (many of them had been in this area before joining the MBA program). The corporate sharks had very busy lives, large salaries but a lack of personal fulfilment. They were often looking for a relationship. There was a minority of corporate seahorses, people who had different positions and then resigned to start their own companies. They were much more motivated than the others but they were tackling the tough learning curve of entrepreneurship. They were not making a fortune, but their wills were awakened and they didn't want to go back to the old system.

One interesting observation from the turtles and sharks was that they had many consultants producing reports for their respective organisations. These reports cost the organisations on average $400 000 and most felt that they changed the status quo very little, nor added value to the organisations they worked for.

I saw how our TSSD model could be applied to our clients, and to other consulting companies, for that matter. Most consultants are either turtles or sharks. As turtles, nothing changes because they provide reports which do not rock the boat. As sharks, most of the larger consulting companies charge a lot of money and introduce some cost-cutting exercises which are supposed to save money in the short term, but do little to preserve or build upon the corporate culture of their clients. There are some rare seahorse consultants who are in niche markets and provide creative ideas to their clients, but they don't really change the whole organisation.

The need for dolphin consultants is becoming a critical issue in order to stop the vicious circle of high consulting fees aiming at downsizing without adding real value to an organisation (shark consultants) while turtle consultants manage the status quo. Our work on building corporate communities is becoming a key issue in order to make a real difference on the planet. Our corporate dolphin consulting pod is growing in Australia, and soon globally.

12

THE VISION BECOMING A REALITY

DOLPHIN WITHIN TRANSFORMATIONS

The participants who join us for the Dolphin Within program are increasingly coming for therapy and self-discovery rather than just being with the dolphins. It is clear that as the research results are spread, more and more people are going to come and the mission will be even more fulfilling for us.

We received a call from a TV reporter, Chris, from Channel 9 in Sydney, who wanted to do a story about the Dolphin Society. Through the Salvation Army, whose workers had already been on the trip, we invited a street kid, Mel. Through a psychotherapist friend, we also invited a young medical student, Tamara, who suffers chronic back pain from an accident several years earlier. The TV crew (three big guys — Chris, Scott and Glenn) joined us for the two days, sailing in the dolphins' environment, learning the dolphins' way of living together and exploring the Dolphin Within.

Through the process, we all started to relate to each other on a very deep level and by the end of the second night, as we were sitting around the campfire, Mel stood up and started to share more about her life. She said that when she wakes up in the mornings, she doesn't want to be here, she stays inside and doesn't want to be with anyone. She said how much she hates society and this world. The journalist asked her whether she would like to have children one day. Mel said no, then she added: 'I've had two children already; one when I was 14 and one when I was 16. They are with foster families now. I've never seen them'. After a long silence, she finally added: 'The first one was from my father, and the second one was from my brother'.

Silence followed, we all knew that something special had happened (in French we says 'an angel is passing') even if we could not put into words. Mel had expressed her biggest pain. She did it in front of the fire and under a beautiful starry sky. Mel had moved all of us, too.

The following morning, Mel and I went for an early walk along the beach. As I was picking up all the plastic bags and bottles along the beach, she was collecting cuttlefish bone for her pet bird. She shared her dream of becoming a welfare worker and helping more children. She said that most of the social workers have a textbook knowledge and do not know how to deal with them. She has an insight, she has been through everything herself. She knows where they are coming from.

We did not managed to swim with dolphins that weekend because the wind was so strong, around 30 to 40 knots. In the middle of the storm, Mel and I were at the bow laughing and shouting at each big wave; the dolphins came to the bow to say hello.

In their last interview, Chris asked Mel if she was disappointed about not swimming with the dolphins. Mel★ said not really, she said how much she got out of the weekend by meeting people who are different from anyone she had met before. She wrote in the *Sirius* guest book: 'I love you both, thanks for changing my life.'

Chris shared the report with us in the spa, his own realisation that this was not a story about dolphins, but about humans. Chris and his team had also been touched. They wrote in the *Sirius* guest book 'moving story, emotional experience'. What showed me how much they have been touched and transformed too was the story of the making of the film.

By the end of the two days, the TV crew offered Mel and Tamara a trip back to Sydney as we had to stay in Port Stephens. That had not been proposed at the beginning of the trip when the issue of the return trip was brought up. It was obvious that as a TV crew, they are used to coming in, shooting, doing the report and getting out the quickest way possible. They not only squeezed all their gear to make room in their car for Mel and Tamara, but, as Mel told me, Chris paid for the dinner when they stopped over and, instead of dropping them at a train station as planned, they gave them a lift all the way home. The Dolphin Within process and Mel's moving story had successfully opened the heart's of these three big guys, which is the best healing they can receive.

We are now running Dolphin Within programs for street kids, autistic kids, and people with AIDS and cancer.

THE DOLPHIN TRIBE

I always knew that Aborigines would play an important role in the Dolphin Society. I thought that when we were ready, they would connect with us. In November 1996, as we were at a festival in Sydney, an Aborigine with long

---

★ Three weeks after the dolphin encounters Mel got a full-time job. She also met a new partner.

white hair and a white beard approached us. He said: 'I am from the Dolphin tribe'.

I was amazed by his eyes and his long white beard. There was some much softness in his eyes. I immediately hugged him and gave him a chain with a dolphin pendant. I knew he was part of the dolphin family. This started a beautiful relationship with a great soul. I learned later that day that he was the famous Burnum Burnum, who, on the 200th anniversary of white settlement in Australia, went to England, put a flag on English soil and read the following declaration:

The Burnum Burnum Declaration
England, 26 January 1988

I, Burnum Burnum, being a nobleman of ancient Australia do hereby take possession of England on behalf of the Aboriginal People.

In claiming outpost, we wish no harm to you natives, but assure you that we are here to bring you good manners, refinement and an opportunity to make a Koopartoo — 'a fresh start'.

Henceforth, an Aboriginal face shall appear on your coins and stamps to signify our sovereignty over this domain.

For the more advanced, we bring the complex language of the Pitjantjatjara; we will teach you how to have a spiritual relationship with the Earth and show you how to get bush tucker.

We do not intend to souvenir, pickle and preserve the heads of 2000 of your people, nor to publicly display the skeletal remains of your Royal Highness, as was done to our Queen Truganinni for 80 years. Neither do we intend to poison your waterholes, lace your flour with strychnine or introduce you to highly toxic drugs.

Based on our 50 000-year heritage, we acknowledge the need to preserve the Caucasian race as of interest to antiquity, although we may be inclined to conduct experiments by measuring the size of your skulls for levels of intelligence. We pledge not to sterilise your women, nor to separate your children from their families.

We give an absolute undertaking that you shall not be placed onto the mentality of government handouts for the next five generations but you will enjoy the full benefits of Aboriginal equality.

At the end of two hundred years, we will make a Treaty to validate occupation by peaceful means and not by conquest.

Finally, we solemnly promise not to make a quarry of England and export your valuable minerals back to the old country, Australia, and we vow never to destroy three quarters of your trees, but to encourage Earth Repair Action to unite people, communities, religions and nations in a common, productive, peaceful purpose.

Burnum Burnum joined the Dolphin Society committee. He came several times to our dolphin nights and brought each time, through his story telling, a very deep experience for everyone. He always said that he felt at home with the dolphin people. I could understand how much he had suffered for being part of the stolen generation and having difficulties reconnecting with his Aboriginal culture. He was torn between two cultures. He devoted his life to being a bridge between the two cultures, but he often felt rejected by both of them. Burnum Burnum belongs to the dolphin tribe, beyond skin colours, cultures, languages, gender.

William and I had the pleasure of visiting his home, and met his wife Marelle, and young son Umbarra.

On Monday 18 August 1997, Burnum Burnum left the physical world after a heart attack following by-pass surgery. His funerals were a symbol of the dream of his whole life: people from all background came together to share how much meeting Burnum Burnum had changed their life. Aborigines and white people alike were united, sharing the same love for his great soul. Burnum has finally stopped fighting and found a way to achieve his mission. His friend reported that Burnum joked: 'is it possible to by-pass a by-pass?' It was sad to see that he had to be dead to finally receive the respect he deserved.

I feel very committed to carrying on his work of reconciliation and I see the dolphins playing an important role in bringing together people from all different cultures beyond religion and differences.

Burnum Burnum's Reconciliation Declaration

Reconciliation by the Nation through Legislation is a worthy Aspiration.
   Its Intention is an Affirmation of Restoration through Mediation and Meditation leading to Self-determination.
   The Equation of Self-determination seeks Definition and Solution by the Coalition.
   Before Reconciliation we had Dispossession, Disruption, Violation, Amalgamation, Annihilation then Protection, Assimilation and Integration.
   Reconciliation implies a Supposition of two Factions in Opposition seeking Options by Caution following Persecution, Exploitation, Isolation, Incarceration, Suppression, Desecration and Incapacitation by one upon the other.
   The 'other' turns the other cheek, rolls with the punches of nature and extends a belated welcome to the Great Southland.

Peace be with you, Burnum Burnum Thanks and love forever.

BILL SMITH

In December 1996, we met with Aboriginal elder, Bill Smith, through a Japanese connection. Nippon TV asked us to be part of a documentary film sponsored by Toshiba. The topic was 'Nature and Technology' and they wanted to film our research program and the Aborigines with the dolphins. My meeting with Bill was an instant heart connection. We invited him and his family aboard *Sirius,* and we had the privilege to visit some of their sacred sites. We are now working on a program where overseas visitors will learn from the dolphins and from Bill and his family, about caring for the land, the oceans and the 'People of the Sea'.

A DOLPHIN CENTRE

When a human enters the water, what becomes apparent is the integral connection between mind and body that the sea forces on her creatures ... The mind enters a different modality where time, weight, and one's self are experienced holistically. In the sea, mind and body become wedded, and the sea's power and lasting steadiness are experienced directly on the skin as well as through the memory banks.

– Joan MacIntyre, 'Mind Play', *Mind in the Waters,* 1974 Project Jonah

Since 1996, we have been working to establish a dolphin centre in Sydney. It will embody and promote a recreational learning lifestyle which will set an appropriate best-practice example of environmentally responsible restoration and preservation, a living example for the future.

The dolphin centre will also be a link back to what the Ancient Greeks called the great river which encircles the world — Oceania. This is where we, people of the land, will once again encounter an ancient friendship with the people of the sea, the dolphins and whales, who guide us back into connection with the ocean realm.

The uniqueness of the centre will be the rich multi-layer experiences which visitors and guests will encounter, ranging from simply dining by the sea to underwater encounters with a friendly wild dolphin.

The Dolphin Society sees Sydney and Australia as playing a key role, leading the world in spreading awareness and educating children, tourists and business people about protection and conservation of whales and dolphins and their marine environment.

The establishment of a dolphin centre in Sydney will spread greater awareness, and will inspire people, organisations and countries to stop mistreating, capturing or killing cetaceans. This is strongly reinforced by Australia's leading role in stopping the needless slaughter of whales worldwide.

In cooperation with Planet Ark, the dolphin centre will take a broader mission in educating the public to 'Save the Planet'.

Planet Ark has considerable expertise in and knowledge of the use of safe products, especially in creating healthy working and living environments with non-toxic, natural materials. This expertise will be brought to bear upon the process of renovating and adapting buildings for the dolphin centre.

With Planet Ark and the Dolphin Society, the dolphin centre will become known worldwide as a dolphin haven: a role model in terms of our handling of the marine environment, biodiversity and human–dolphin interaction. It will also be the place where we train corporate dolphins through management workshops.

The Dolphin Society will run an annual program of conferences, week-long events, international and national events, providing a universally attractive theme: the dolphin lifestyle. The dolphin centre will become known as a place to experience the dolphin approach to life, based on:

- Freedom from stress: personal and environmental health
- Fun: entertaining and enriching experiences
- Cooperation: teamwork and synergy
- Brainpower: optimum use of our brains for peak performance
- Creativity: problem solving
- Exploration of the oceans and people of the sea
- Cultural exchanges for people from Australia and overseas.

People will experience a dolphin lifestyle, a new way of looking at life through dolphins' eyes in terms of personal health, management of the environment and business strategy.

The dolphin centre will showcase individuals and companies who are making a difference, for example waste water management, recycling and clean-up technologies.

Providing dolphin–human encounters
Ultimately, the dolphin centre will become known worldwide as a place where dolphins have freely chosen to visit and interact with people, without feeding programs or captivity. The Dolphin Society will develop human–dolphin encounters through different experiences. Anyone of any age will be able to have a dolphin encounter, many without needing to get wet.

Dolphin interactive learning centre
A dolphin interactive learning centre will be created using interactive devices, sounds and virtual images. It will include: a special effects theatre and cinema, where different films relating to whales, dolphins and the environment will be played each day; an exhibition space where artists of various origins will display works, mainly about dolphins, whales and the ocean; a cetacean library

exhibiting the best books, CDs and videos on dolphins and whales (many will also be sold at the Dolphin Shop); and Dolphin Society Internet access.

The dolphin learning centre will be entertaining for the young, but will have ample research information for the scientifically serious. It will be thematically oriented, containing the following sections:

- Palaeontology — showing the evolution of dolphins, whales and marine mammals in general.
- History — explaining historical relationships between people, dolphins, whales and other marine mammals, including the history of marine mammal hunting that led to its being banned in most of the world in recent years. Particular emphasis will be placed on the history of dolphins and whales in Sydney, NSW and Australia, showing the important role Australia plays in protecting dolphins and whales worldwide.
- Biology — showing the relationship of marine mammals to other marine creatures, as well as details about physiology, reproduction, migration patterns, species, etc.
- Art — dolphins have inspired books, sculptures, paintings, music, and films, which will be displayed in static and interactive ways with the latest technology. There will be a particular emphasis on Aboriginal art, showing artefacts of ancient times, especially those concerned with the dolphin-human connection, the sea and/or the Sydney area.

Marine dolphin experience

An underwater facility will be developed where sounds of dolphins and whales can be transmitted whilst people experience the marine environment through snorkelling and scuba diving. Guests will learn to swim, snorkel and scuba dive in the dolphins' natural environment. Ultimately, wild dolphins will be invited to join of their own free will to meet the people.

Underwater concerts will be regularly conducted there.

Dolphin therapy programs

Specific therapy programs will be provided for people who need emotional and physical healing, for example: street kids, people suffering from drug addiction or suicidal thoughts, autistic kids, depressed people and people suffering from stress.

Dolphin shop

Learning materials such books, posters and videos will be sold to educate people about the beauty and importance of marine mammals and the ocean. Other dolphin and whale-inspired products will be also be sold — with the guiding principle of promoting arts and crafts and the use of natural materials and processes in production.

THE DECLARATION AT THE UNITED NATIONS

Our *Universal Declaration of Marine Mammal Rights* is gathering support and strength all over the world. In just a few months, hundreds of people 'signed' the petition on our Internet page; reading their words of support is a great encouragement to us. It is also heartening how many people want to express their views openly on this issue; the web site has a public petition page where people's comments are automatically registered and displayed for everyone to see. It is a global forum.

We are also gathering signatures of support from people in Australia and in the US where the Declaration was published in a news magazine with a circulation of several hundred thousand. Readers were encouraged to collect signatures themselves, and send them to us. It is this sort of networking and spreading the word that we value the most.

When we have enough signatures of support, we intend to take the Declaration to the United Nations, through Australia's representative, for eventual ratification there. This is the first stage; ultimately we would like to see the Declaration extended beyond cetaceans.

By gathering millions of signatures for the Declaration of Rights, we will be able to act as an 'Amnesty International' for the people of the sea.

DOLPHINS IN THE HARBOUR BY 2000

When we first created the Dolphin Society, we said that we would find a way to facilitate the return of dolphins to Sydney's waters by 2000. After dedicating two years to the research, we started late in 1996 to focus on the Dolphins in the Harbour project. This story, which is unfolding as I write, is another book. However, I can share the beginning of it.

After a particularly vicious speargun attack on Bluey (my dear blue groper), Howie managed to get the local mayor to listen to our concerns. A story appeared in the Sydney newspapers as a result, saying how the mayor wanted to increase protection for Bluey and his friends. We were then contacted by a journalist for a follow-up story on Bluey. He came to our place and we showed him film, photos and articles. The article appeared the next day (Saturday), under the headline 'Chips are Down for Battered Fish'.

Then, in Sunday's paper, a small paragraph appeared quoting none other than the Premier of New South Wales, Bob Carr, who said that he had swum with Bluey and that he wanted to do something about the situation!

I sent a photo of Bluey to Bob Carr with a simple note: 'We have a common friend'. Later I sent him a fax asking for a meeting to talk about protection of Bluey and the dolphins.

A few days later, the Minister for Fisheries, Bob Martin, made an announcement in Clovelly, doubling the fines for spearfishing blue groper from $5000 to $10 000. We thanked him and told him that this was a good first step in getting greater protection along Sydney's urban coastline, but more was needed. We shared our vision to bring dolphins back to Sydney Harbour.

A week later William and I walked into the Premier's office. Bob Carr immediately mentioned that when he was Minister of the Environment he put in place a protection act on dolphins in NSW. We did not have to explain anything about dolphins — he knew. We simply shared our vision to bring dolphins back to Sydney Harbour by 2000. He was very enthusiastic and wanted to become involved.

In December 1996, I co-facilitated a *Dolphins in the Harbour* workshop for 70 people. We joined forces with Planet Ark. The workshop gathered together 70 stakeholders of Sydney Harbour — politicians, bureaucrats, environmentalists, scientists and business people — to share our vision and create a strategic action plan. Bob Carr opened the workshop for us.

By facilitating the return of dolphins to Sydney Harbour, the Dolphin Society and Planet Ark will create a unique event in human–dolphin encounters. This will attract global media attention to Sydney and set a world model, a best practice for human–dolphin encounters. In terms of dolphin therapy we will show that we do not need to have dolphins in captivity. It is much better to create a clean and safe habitat for them, so that dolphins can initiate encounters with humans on their terms.

The *Dolphins in the Harbour* initiative is not just about dolphins. It aims to: educate the citizenry to 'think dolphin' and become conscious of the value of water resources; promote sustainable harbour management as a model for other harbour cities; and create a 'sisterhood' of harbour cities around the world.

After the workshop, *The Sydney Morning Herald's* headline was: 'Healthy harbour to be a dolphin haven' (Bob Beale, *Sydney Morning Herald,* 11 December 1996). Since the workshop we have worked closely with government and businesses to help solve the issues of clean water, fish stocks and human activities in the harbour. The project has already attracted interest from other harbour cities in the world for twin projects.

In March 1997, the front page of the *Sydney Morning Herald* announced:

War on harbour pollution — a budget push to clean up sewage and stormwater overflows

Environmental groups began a campaign recently to refocus attention on the pollution of waterways and called for Government reforms that would return dolphins to the harbour as a symbol of improved water quality.

(Mark Riley and David Humphries, *Sydney Morning Herald*, 15 March 1997)

The budget was announced a few weeks later: '$3bn waterway clean up for 2000'. Bob Carr's vision was expressed: 'I want my legacy as a Premier to be the saving of the State's forests and the cleaning up of the State's waterways.' (Mark Riley, *Sydney Morning Herald*, 2 May 1997.)

A dolphin in the political world!

THE WATER CRISIS

Through the Dolphins in the Harbour project, we learnt the following:

1. The world's sewage and stormwater systems have changed little since Roman times. This technology uses many kilometres of underground pipes and channels that run into the rivers and oceans. With continued urban development these pipes are discharging more and more polluted water into rivers and oceans all over the world.

2. Stormwater run-off is becoming the critical issue of urban marine pollution. The urban environment has created impermeable surfaces with concrete roads, parking spaces and roofs. These surfaces increase water run-off from about 10% (in undeveloped areas) to 90% (in cities). Our cities are like a cancer for our rivers and oceans.

3. Water is the most precious resource in the world, and we are wasting it. There are already wars about water and predictions say there will be even more by the year 2012. According to Time Magazine's Special Issue, November 1997:

'The stark truth is that in much of the world there isn't enough water, and where there is, it is being wasted, mismanaged and polluted on a grand scale. According to an April report from the United Nations and the Stockholm Environment Institute, by the year 2025, two-third of the world's population will be affected by. water shortages. In 1995, 20% of the planet's people already had no access to clean drinking water and 50% lacked proper toilet facilities. "The world has got a very big water problem", says Sir Tickell, former British ambassador to the U.N. and one of the organisers of the 1992 Earth Summit in Rio de Janeiro. "It will be the progenitor of more wars than oil. World demand for water doubles every 21 years, but the volume available is the same as it was in Roman times. Something has got to give'.

What we need in a paradigm shift in terms of water management: a new way of managing water by working with nature rather than against it. We need more permeable surfaces in our cities: gardens, roof gardens, roads with plants and trees to maximise infiltration. We need the water to percolate through soils to become clean and we need storage systems so we can re-use the water.

OPEN TO SURPRISE

The mission of ODB Consulting will be to develop more and more corporate dolphins. In doing so, ODB will develop more and more corporate dolphin consultants. It does not mean that we will be a huge and global consulting company, but rather a network of consultants who share similar values and receive and use the Delphi process.

William and I will always be open to surprises. We know that the dolphins will lead us towards new territories and that we cannot yet comprehend the new dimensions we are going to explore. I know that part of the plan is the creation of a fiction film, as it is the quickest way to share the dolphin message on a global scale. I know that this film will involve my two brothers (Henry is working for the Cousteau Society based in the South Pacific), so we will all meet again in the Mediterranean.

THE DOLPHINS, OUR TEACHERS

We are aware that through the Dolphin Within program, we are ourselves trained and transformed by the dolphins. Each time we swim with them, we learn to be more our true selves. The more we become different from each other, as William and Olivia, experiencing our respective individuality, the more we connect with each other, the more we respect each other and love each other unconditionally.

When I come back on the yacht after a swim with the dolphins, I often cannot talk. I cannot even find words now to describe this state. You might think, I have just written a whole book about it, but I would like to finish up with the experience without analyses. My dream is to have, one day, a video camera on top of my head, in order to capture what I see. Until that time, please imagine...

- Three dolphins swimming below you, in circle and turning slightly to make eye contact with you and smile at you. They are not just swimming below you, they are looking up at you, looking through you with their eyes and sonar and inviting you to play and join them below.

- Holding hands with two men in the water, and as you look down under, you see three dolphins coming straight towards you, looking at you and waiting for you to follow them in a synchronised dance.
- Swimming like a dolphin with two other women, and you can hear the clicks and high-pitched sounds like a laugh, telling you, 'that's good, you are learning'. As you all swim together under water, suddenly three dolphins appear from the side and come straight in front of all of you, one for each of you.
- You drive on a road south of Melbourne and see a group of people by the beach; it is winter. As you approach closely, you are told that there is a sick dolphin in the bay. Imagine that you get your fins and mask and enter the cold water. Imagine that you can hear the dolphin sounds as you swim toward him and that you manage to take him in your arms. Imagine that as you hold him warm against you, you suddenly realise that he is dying in your arms ... he was waiting for a presence to let his spirit leave his body.
- You are meditating in a marina, preparing for a workshop involving a large number of business people. Imagine that you ask for help and as you open your eyes, a dolphin enters the marina, swimming straight towards you.
- You live in Sydney and go swimming every morning in front of your house. Imagine that as you are sitting on the beach you close your eyes and think, 'one day, as I open my eyes, the dolphins will be there'. Then you open your eyes, that day, more than twenty dolphins are in the bay in front of you.
- You are on a yacht and start calling the dolphins, which are far away. You start seeing the large pod rushing in your direction; as they come closer and closer you jump into the water; the large pod of dolphins comes straight to you, passing centimetres away, blasting you with their sounds.
- You start to send messages to dolphins through visual images and realise that the dolphins respond to you...
- Someone is playing the didgeridoo at the bow of the yacht and a dolphin comes from far away, right alongside the yacht, and places his nose under the didgeridoo.
- A sunset and you are swimming like a dolphin toward the orange light, surrounded and followed by a pod of twenty dolphins.

This is a small snapshot of my adventures, and I feel absolutely privileged to have been accepted in the dolphins' world. You may by now understand why I have dedicated my life to finding ways to share and bring these experiences and this state of consciousness to more people.

I often think if only more people could know that life can be so beautiful, that being human is about feeling that state rather than the limitations, reactions, pain and competitiveness, the world would be so different.

THE WORLD TO COME

My heart surgery with the dolphins was an opening of my 'heart centre' where there are, according to esoteric texts, the most refined etheric substances, the most refined degree of the life force, the gold of the alchemists. Such opening of the heart allows the inner self to shine: 'the heart becomes the flame that can resonate with Angels'.

What I have learnt from the dolphins is unconditional love. It is beyond the emptiness of spirit that humans usually experience (the personal stage — the shark/seahorse way). It is not what children experience when they are bathing in the web of love (the pre-personal stage — the turtle way). It is not only enlightenment coming from outside, it is not only a merging, a dissolving of the ego, a total being with divinity described by some Indian schools of meditation or esoteric tradition. The experience of love with the dolphins is a transformation coming from inside, from *within*. It gave me a clear sense of 'I am', a strong sense of self and uniqueness of my purpose.

What I have been observing and developing in the dolphin environment is a field of energy, a web of energy, a matrix for feeling (not emotional shark or seahorse reactions). In this field, dolphins are catalysts for human transformation. It is a space of 'heartness', where humans can experience their capacity for unconditional love. In this field, humans learn to connect with this web, the web of love that can unify human beings.

My purpose on the planet is to be, like the dolphins, a 'heart surgeon' for human transformation. The power of love is the only power I use in my relationships, my research, my therapy work, my corporate consulting work. In anything we do, we create this field of a certain frequency which allow humans to experience unconditional love, to connect with the web of love and awaken to their full potential.

I have seen hundreds of humans been zapped by dolphin love, been transformed by their eyes, their sounds, and their energy — and I keep thinking: 'If they can do it, why can't I do it too, why can't we all do it' — this might be the real human adventure, the true reason for our existence on this planet.

The world to come is a world where more and more people will be reaching this transpersonal stage — and will be evolving in that web of love. It might take many generations, it might take eons, it is up to each of us!

BIBLIOGRAPHY

DOLPHIN BOOKS

This is a selected list, with comments, of our dolphin library. It covers the areas of dolphins, business and brain. For more information on books on dolphins, I encourage you to consult, as I did, Trisha Lamb Feuerstein's web site (www.dreamgate.com/asd-13/4r30.htm#10) where she has a complete bibliography and filmography on dolphins and whales.

CARWARDINE, MARK. *Whales, Porpoises & Dolphins: The Visual Guide to All the World's Cetaceans.* London/New York: Dorling Kindersby, 1995. An Eyewitness handbook.

• The most comprehensive pocket guide to cetaceans of the world with more than 900 illustrations, an authoritative text, detailed illustrations, and a systematic approach. It enable us to recognise each species quickly and easily.

COCHRANE, AMANDA, and CALLEN, KARENA. *Dolphins and Their Power to Heal.* Rochester, Vermont: Healing Arts Press/London: Bloomsbury, 1992.

• This is the best summary of the current 'dolphin phenomenon'. Amanda (whom we met in London in June 1996) and Karena relate myths and legends from the world over that attest to the healing influence that dolphins have on humans. They relate recent case studies where close contact dolphins trigger human inherent healing powers. They also explore the dolphins' life cycle, behavioural patterns, and methods of communication, dolphin midwives, dolphin intelligence and much more.

COUSTEAU, JACQUES-YVES. *Dolphins.* New York: A & W Visual Publishers, 1975.

• The twenty-five years of the Cousteau adventure on board the Calypso, encountering dolphins in the open seas.

DOAK, WADE. *Friends in the Sea.* Auckland, New Zealand: Hodder Moa Beckett Publishers, 1995.

• Doak describes the interactions between solo wild dolphins and people in New Zealand and Australia.

DOAK, WADE. *Swimming with Dolphins in New Zealand.* Auckland: Hodder & Stoughton, 1994.

• Doak presents Project Interlock, a global network he set up with his wife, Jan, to learn about dolphins in the wild. He reveals unforgettable encounters between humans and dolphins in New Zealand.

DOAK, WADE. *Encounters with Whales and Dolphins.* Auckland: Hodder & Stoughton, 1988.

• Wade and Jan devoted themselves to exploring the cetacean mind through communication such as the mimetic use of the dolphin suit, music and creative play, and found that dolphins extend their signalling systems to humans. They researched the histories of 30 solitary dolphins that have sought human companionship for prolonged periods. They discovered remote and special dolphin tribes in close rapport with humans in the Bahamas, Brazil and Australia. They found whales just as ready to communicate.

DOAK, WADE. *Dolphin, Dolphin.* New York: Sheridan House, 1980.

• In 1975, following an encounter with dolphins, Wade and Jan sold their house and bought a Polynesian catamaran which they transformed into a research vessel. Project Interlock was born to study dolphin-initiated approaches to human, opening fascinating future possibilities.

DOBBS, HORACE. *Journey into Dolphin Dreamtime.* London: Jonathan Cape, 1992.

• Part three of the trilogy, the other two being *Tale of Two Dolphins* and *Dance to a Dolphin's Song.* Horace relates his voyage of discovery with Aborigines in Australia; Freddie, the Amble dolphin; JoJo, the Caribbean dolphin; and the first Dolphin Therapy Centre in Japan.

DOBBS, HORACE. *Save the Dolphins.* London: Souvenir Press, 1992.

• Horace relates the life of the dolphin Donald until his mysterious disappearance. Horace calls for the freedom of all dolphins. He takes us around the world discovering dolphins in the wild and in captivity. He recounts the anguish of the Iki Island dolphin massacre and the joy of Rocky's successful release from the Morecambe dolphinarium.

DOBBS, HORACE. *Dance to a Dolphin's Song: The Story of a Quest for the Magic Healing Power of the Dolphin.* London: Jonathan Cape, 1990.

• (Grew out of two television films: *Bewitched by a Dolphin* and *The Dolphin's Touch.*) Horace tells the story of Simo, a wild dolphin who lived near Solva in Pembrokeshire, and Funghie, the famous Dingle Dolphin, and the people whose lives were changed by their experiences with these dolphins.

DOBBS, HORACE. *Follow a Wild Dolphin: The Story of an Extraordinary Friendship.* Dobbs Ferry, N.Y.: Sheridan House, 1990/London: Souvenir Press, 1990.

• Horace relates his life-changing friendship with Donald and Percy, two wild dolphins off the coast of Cornwall; his interaction with wild dolphins off the coast of Ireland; his experience of dolphins in Florida associating with humans in 'open confinement', and his encounter with JoJo, a wild bottlenose dolphin in the Turks and Caicos Islands.

DOBBS, HORACE. *The Magic of Dolphins.* Guildford, England: Lutterworth Press/Dobbs Ferry, N.Y.: Sheridan House, 1990.

DOBBS, HORACE. *Tale of Two Dolphins.* London: Jonathan Cape, 1987.

• Horace relates how the gentle dolphin, Percy, helps a woman who could not swim yet to be courageous enough to get into the sea. This remarkable encounter led Horace to set up Operation Sunflower, a research project which investigates the uplifting effect of dolphins on the human spirit. Horace also describes his encounter with Jean Louis, a lone female dolphin off Brittany.

FICHTELIUS, KARL-ERIK, and **SJOLANDER, SVERRE.** *Smarter than Man? Intelligence in Whales, Dolphins and Humans.* New York: Pantheon Books/Random House, 1972.

• A Swedish professor of medicine, Dr Fichtelius, has spent five years studying and communicating with dolphins. He presents a comparative study of large-brained animals, using recent scientific findings, and shows that in many areas the intelligence of whales and dolphins are superior to those of humans.

HAYTER, ADRIAN. *The Dolphins' Message.* A. Hayter, 1981.

JOHNSON, JESSICA, and **ODENT, MICHEL.** *We are All Water-Babies.* London: Dragon's World, 1994; Berkeley, CA: Ten Speed Press, 1995.

• Jessica Johnson and Dr Michel Odent describe the relationship of humans with water, its special role during pregnancy, and the link with dolphins.

LILLY, JOHN C. *The Scientist: A Novel Autobiography.* New York: Bantam, 1978, 1981.

• In his autobiography, Lilly covers his early experimentation with dolphins and includes a chapter entitled 'Simulation of the Future of Man, Dolphin, and Whale'.

LILLY, JOHN C *Communication Between Man and Dolphin: The Possibility of Talking with Other Species.* New York: Julian Press, 1978.

• Lilly relates his research results of through 1978, describes the programs he is currently undertaking, and predicts potential relationships between humans and dolphins.

LILLY, JOHN C. *Lilly on Dolphins: Humans of the Sea.* Garden City, New York: Anchor Press/ Doubleday, 1975.

• This book includes *Man and Dolphin* (shortened version), The Mind of the Dolphin: A Non-Human Intelligence, Lilly's lecture 'Modern Whales, Dolphins, and Porpoises', Challenges to Our Intelligence, from The Dolphin in History, and other scientific papers, extensive bibliographies, and an index.

LILLY, JOHN C. *The Mind of the Dolphin: A Nonhuman Intelligence.* New York: Doubleday and Company, 1967.

• Lilly details, in his progress report, the discoveries about the dolphin's abilities, current ideas about his intellect, and the paradoxes of inter-species communication, developed since 1961. He underlines the astonishing intricacy and nonhuman nature of the dolphin's intelligence and yet the profound relevance of that intelligence to man's place in Nature.

LILLY, JOHN C. *Man and Dolphin.* New York: Doubleday and Company, 1961.

• In this work, Lilly made his famous prediction that: 'Within the next decade or two the human species will establish communication with another species: nonhuman, alien, possibly extraterrestrial, more probably marine. And we may encounter ideas, philosophies, ways and means not previously conceived in the minds of men'.

MAYOL, JACQUES. Homo Delphinus, Glenat, 1986.

• French book which relates Jacques' extraordinary research in apneic (breath-holding) demonstrating humanity's dual origin from the sea and the womb.

MCINTYRE, JOAN. *The Delicate Art of Whale Watching.* San Francisco: Sierra Club Books, 1982.

• For five years Joan headed a well-known group working to understand and protect cetaceans [Project Jonah]; then, wanting to be physically closer to her subjects, she moved to a remote Pacific island, a place where whales and dolphins are seasonal visitors. In this book, she shares many of her experiences.

MCINTYRE, JOAN. *Mind in the Waters: A Book to Celebrate the Consciousness of Whales.* New York: Scribners/San Francisco: Sierra Club, 1974.

• Through mythology as well as scientific finds, poetry as well as natural history, statistics as well as photographs, *Mind in the Waters* lead us into the celebration of whale and dolphin consciousness. This extraordinary collection of many contributing writers, poets, and scientists fulfils our scientific mind, our heart and our soul.

NOLLMAN, JIM. *Dolphin Dreamtime: The Art and Science of Interspecies Communication.* New York: Bantam, 1987.

• Jim, an internationally known pioneer in interspecies communication, describes his experiences with animals using music as a common language. This extraordinary musician and ecologist talks with dolphins, seagulls, whales, buffalo, bears, and even a mosquito. Jim gives us dramatic examples of our evolving relationship with the animal kingdom and draws on ecology, zoology, mythology, and shamanism to awaken us to rethink our ideas about animal consciousness.

O'BARRY, RICK, with COULBOURN, KEITH. *Behind the Dolphin Smile.* Chapel Hill, North Carolina: Algonquin Books, 1989.

• Rick describes how he started working with captive dolphins, including his employment as television star Flipper's trainer, and his personal realisation of the horror of dolphins in captivity.

OCEAN, JOAN. *Dolphin Connection: Inter-dimensional Ways of Living.* Kailua-Kona, Hawaii/Fitzroy, Australia: Dolphin Connection/Spiral, 1989.

• Joan describes how she experiences a human—dolphin communication that releases expansive, multi-sensory knowledge in the entire body and its thoughtforms.

ODENT, MICHEL. *Water and Sexuality.* New York: Penguin/Arkana, 1990.

• Dr Michel Odent brings an interesting comparison of humans, apes, and dolphins which shows that humans have many characteristics more similar to dolphins than to apes. The basis of the aquatic ape theory.

PAYNE, ROGER. *Among Whales.* New York: Charles Scribner's Sons, 1995/Toronto: Maxwell Macmillan Canada, 1993.

• Roger Payne is described as a scientist, an activist and a romantic, an explorer, and a musician. So his book is a work of biology — cetacean, marine, and human; of exploration, of sociology, of cultural mythology, of philosophy, and of literature. It addresses a broad range of important questions such as: What is the device by which whales sing, and why do they do it? For what purposes do dolphins use their large and complex brains? What is the purpose of the human brain?

PAYNE, ROGER, ed. *Communication and Behaviour of Whales.* Boulder, Colorado: Westview Press, 1983.

ROBSON, FRANK. *Thinking Dolphins, Talking Whales.* Wellington, New Zealand: AH & AW Reed, 1976.

• The New Zealand coast has unusual numbers of whale strandings. Tackling the question of why they strand leads Frank into some incredible situations and gives us some surprising answers.

PAYNE, ROGER. *Pictures in the Dolphin Mind.* Auckland, New Zealand: Reed Methuen/Dobbs Ferry, N.Y.: Sheridan House, 1988.

• Frank gives reasons for the mass strandings and practical advice on assisting beached whales. He also offers us insights about his gifted way to communicate with cetaceans.

SIFAOUI, BRIGITTE. *Le Livre des Dauphins et des Baleines.* C.L.E.S. - Albin Michel, 1996.

• Brigitte gives us more than 1000 contacts and ideas to meet, protect and communicate with whales and dolphins. Brigitte's book is the first to mention the work of the Dolphin Society.

STENUIT, ROBERT. *The Dolphin, Cousin to Man.* New York: Bantam, 1972.

TENZIN-DOLMA, LISA. *The Dolphin Experience.* London/New York: Foulsham, 1992.

• After a brief introduction to the natural history of dolphins, their interactions with humans, and dolphin mythology, Lisa relates thirteen personal accounts of interaction with primarily the lone wild dolphin Fungie (the 'Dingle Dolphin'). She concludes with a consideration of ecology and conservation issues.

WEYLER, REX. *Song of the Whale.* Anchor Press, 1986.

• Paul Spong's true-life adventures with killer whales are related by journalist Rex Weyler. Everything starts with a scientific quest for knowledge and leads to a heroic crusade to save these fascinating creatures from extinction. Paul and his Orca lab leads world non-intrusive research into cetaceans in the wild.

WYLLIE, TIMOTHY. *Dolphins, Telepathy & Underwater Birthing: Further Adventures among Spiritual Intelligences.* Santa Fe, New Mexico: Bear & Co., 1993.

WYLLIE, TIMOTHY. *Dolphins, ETs & Angels: Adventures among Spiritual Intelligences.* Santa Fe, New Mexico: Bear & Co., 1984.

• Timothy's adventure is full of surprises and gives us magical encounters with Australian Aborigines, New Zealand Maoris, an American walk-in, a Russian midwife, and a Balinese shaman. He explores the spiritual nature of dolphins, their involvement with underwater birthing, and the nature of dolphin telepathic communication.

CORPORATE DOLPHIN BOOKS

ADLER, NANCY J. *International Dimensions of Organisational Behaviour.* Boston: PWS-KENT Publishing Company, 1991.

• A very insightful book about global organisations.

BELBIN MEREDITH R. *Management Teams, Why they Succeed or Fail.* London: Butterworth Heinemann, 1981.

• A key research book and an instrument for understanding the dynamics of a team.

COLLINS & CHIPPENDALE. *New Wisdom II, Values-Based Development.* Brisbane: ACORN Publications, 1995.

• Precious research on values and brain dominance.

GLASER, CONNIE, and SMALLEY, BARBARA STEINBERG. *Swim With the Dolphins: How Women Can Succeed in Corporate America on Their Own Terms.* New York: Warner Books, 1995.

• A collection of case studies of women in business using the dolphin approach. Very surprisingly the book does not refer to Dudley Lynch's book *Strategy of the Dolphin* (q.v.) which is certainly the original model for it.

HOFSTEDE, GEERT. *Cultures and Organisations, Software of the Mind, Intercultural Cooperation and its Importance for Survival.* London: McGraw-Hill, 1991.

• An important insight about culture as a conditioning of the mind, and its impact on business.

LYNCH, DUDLEY, and KORDIS, PAUL. *DolphinThink: The Workbook.* Brain Technologies, 1989.

LYNCH, DUDLEY, and KORDIS, PAUL. *Strategy of the Dolphin.* New York: Fawcett-Columbine, 1988.

• The management book which inspires me the most. It allows me to bring the dolphin message into the business world. I recommend it for everyone, not just corporate people, as a way to understand how to become human dolphins.

OHMAE, KENICHI. *The Borderless World.* UK: Collins, 1990.

• A business book which gives some key about the emerging global village and the resultant melting away of national economic borders.

RODDICK, ANITA. *Body and Soul.* Ebury Press, 1991.

• The story of a Corporate Seahorse, the creator of the Body Shop.

SCHIEN, EDGAR H. *Process Consulting.* Volume I and II, USA: Addison-Wesley, 1988.

• The basis of our consulting approach, as process consultants we focus jointly on diagnosis and on the passing on to the client of our diagnostic skills.

SENGE, PETER. *The Fifth Discipline.* New York: Random House, 1990.

• The learning organisation in detail.

WHEATLEY, MARGARET J. *Leadership and the New Science.* California: Berrett-Koehler, 1992.

• An application of quantum physic to the business world.

DOLPHIN SPIRITUAL BOOKS

DEAN, STANLEY R, editor. *Psychiatry and Mysticism*. Chicago: Nelson-Hall, 1975.

FROMM, ERICH. *The Art of Loving (l'Art d'Aimer)*. Editions de l'Epi, Paris, 1956.

MORGAN, MARLO. *Mutant Message Downunder,* Macmillan, 1991

SAGAN, SAMUEL. *Awakening the Third Eye.* Sydney: Clairvision School Press, 1992.

SAGAN, SAMUEL. *Atlantean Secrets.* Sydney: Clairvision School Press, 1996.

WILBER, KEN. *The Atman Project.* Quest Books, Wheaton USA, 1980.

• An introduction to transpersonal psychology.

DOLPHIN BRAIN BOOKS

CADE, C. MAXWELL, and COXHEAD, NONA. *The Awakened Mind.* New York: Delacorte Press, 1979.

• An excellent book on higher state of consciousness.

HUTCHISON, MICHAEL. *Mega Brain Power.* New York: Hyperion, 1994.

• A good summary of the research on brain technology and its implication for alpha and theta training.

GROF, S. *Beyond the Brain.* New York State: University of New York Press, 1985.

GREGORY, R. *The Oxford Companion to the Mind.* Oxford University Press, 1987.

• A dictionary of useful terms related to the mind.

NIEDERMEYER, ERNEST and LOPES DA SILVA, FERNANDO. *Electroencephalography, Basic Principles, Clinical Applications, and Related Fields.* Third edition, Maryland, USA: Williams & Wilkins, 1993.

• A mine of information — more than one thousand pages — on EEG research.

DOLPHIN WITHIN LANGUAGE

A Glossary of terms used in Dolphin Within work

Archetype — The perfect prototype. Once created, all things and beings evolve towards the perfection of their archetype. We call the archetype of each individual their 'full potential', or their 'Dolphin Within'.

Astral Body — The vehicle of emotions and thoughts. Whenever we think or experience an emotion, something is taking place in our astral body.

Awakening — Rousing, reanimating, reviving. We see a Dolphin Within experience as a catalyst, a process of awakening people to their full potential.

Beingness — A state of pure being. A pure form of consciousness, in which there is just being. One is, and that is it.

Big Blue — The depths of the ocean, a way to reach the cosmic divinity, a state of peace. Also the famous film by Luc Besson which portrays Jacques Mayol's life story (highly recommended viewing).

Brainwaves - Electrical activity in the brain as measured with an electroencephalograph (EEG).

Chakras — Sanskrit term for 'wheels', hypothetical centres of radiation of primal energy (prana). Most systems distinguish seven chakras: anal, genital, navel, heart, throat, brow and crown.

Dolphin Assisted Beingness — The essential purpose of the process is to 'be more'. It is common to hear that human beings are only using a small fraction of their potential. Dolphin Within beingness is an experience which assists humans to be more in touch with their full potential.

Dolphin Assisted Therapy (DAT) — A therapy which involves encounters with dolphins. The Dolphin Society does not condone any DAT involving dolphins in captivity. Our research shows that dolphin therapy in the wild is even more powerful.

Dolphin Charter — The Dolphin Society's Declaration of Rights for Marine Mammals, which is an extension of the *Universal Declaration of Human Rights* to the 'People of the Sea'.

Dolphin Drunkenness — A laughing and happy state which often follows a dolphin experience. The laughing is very contagious and can last a long time. People are high on Spirit, rather than any external substance.

Dolphin Evening — A monthly evening held at Hugh and Philip's Café in Sydney, where Dolphin Society people meet to share research results and dolphin stories. The evening is open to everyone.

Dolphin Pod — Each Dolphin Within trip creates a team or pod of individuals who share deep experience and become friends for life. They share the Dolphin Within learning, values and Charter, and respect for the dolphins.

Dolphin Society — A non-profit organisation founded in October 1994, dedicated to the research of the healing power of dolphins, the creation of Dolphin Therapy Centres and the conservation and protection of dolphins and whales.

Dolphin Therapy Centre — A centre which uses, in conjunction with other therapies, encounters of dolphins in the wild, or simulated encounters through multimedia effects (dolphin sounds diffused through water in the ocean or a swimming pool, films, music, or virtual reality).

Dolphin Swim — A swim style which simulates the dolphin's way of moving in the water. The legs stay in close contact with each other, the arms are along the body. Dolphins respond very well to such non-verbal styles of communication.

Dolphin Thinking — A different mode of thinking, not based on reaction or conditioning. It does not appear like a mechanical chain of reactions, but like a creative activity of the soul in which the heart plays a central role; Thinking and Self are married in the heart.

Dolphin Within Experience/State — A theta brainwave frequency (alpha/theta brainwave and awakened mind) which corresponds to an experience of the higher self, one's full potential or the archetype.

Dolphin Within Pattern — Psychological and emotional improvements which have been repeatedly observed with the 240 or so people who have experienced their 'Dolphin Within'. Examples are freedom from addiction, depression, or stress.

Dolphin Within Values — Integrity, dedication to truth, vision, opening, joy and enthusiasm.

Dolphinicity — 'Dolphinicity is the magic beyond synchronicity, which is more than coincidence' (Estelle Myers).

Echolocation — The dolphin way of perceiving and communicating through high-frequency sound or ultrasound.

Ego, Higher Self and Spirit — Facets of the divine side of human nature, as opposed to the little ego or the astral body (emotions and thoughts).

Electroencephalograph (EEG) — A machine which allows the measurement of electrical impulses created by the brain.

Enlightenment — A state of union with the Divine. There are different paths of enlightenment.

Etheric Body — The layer of life force. Equated with the Qi of Chinese medicine. When we feel a vibration through the body (for example a 'zapping' by a dolphin's sonar), it means that something has been activated in our etheric body.

Field — A space in which an energy is held. We see Port Stephens as a bay where, like the dolphins, we interact with a special field which is a catalyst for transformation.

Healing — In our parlance, healing is connecting people with their higher self. Our approach to therapy and consulting is not a quick fix, but provides a healing or learning space for people to see their higher self and find their own truth.

Higher Purpose — Our 'raison d'être' on Earth. Each individual has a dream to bring into reality. The key is to find it, and to be committed to following it through.

Homo Delphinus — A term created by the French diver, our great friend, Jacques Mayol, who is the subject of the film *The Big Blue*, which describes the evolution of *Homo sapiens* towards the dolphin state.

Human Dolphins — People who can self-regulate their brains and easily access beta, alpha and theta brainwaves at will, to reach peak performance. They can also access the awakened mind pattern. People who are in touch with their higher self, their full potential. They have explored their turtle, shark and seahorse characters. They know their purpose and do not react, but flow with life.

Human Potential — It is common to hear that humans under-utilise their brain. Human life is confined with a limited range of thoughts, emotions, sensations and other modalities of conscious existence and yet, in most cases, they remain completely unaware of these limitations.

Human Seahorses — People who primarily access alpha and theta brainwaves. They are very creative and their main motivation is to be different. Their main reaction is flight. A seahorse is one of the two characters of the personal stage; the one that demonstrates a lot of individualism and self-expression.

Human Sharks — People who primarily live in beta brainwaves, whose main reaction is to fight. A shark is one of the two characters of the personal stage, the one which demonstrate a lot of will.

Human Turtle — People who have no dominant brainwaves. Their main reaction is to freeze. Turtles have the features of the pre-personal stage, bathing in cosmic divinity but with no self, without the will of the shark or the individualism of the seahorse.

Marguerite Flower — Term for the observed behaviour of the sperm whale (*Physeter macrocephalus*) when they make a circle in the water, with their heads pointing inwards on the shape of a flower. Imagine the biggest brains on the planet meeting together in this way. The legend says that the Marguerite Flower is a way for the whales to bring the Word of the God down to the Earth, and that the dolphins are the messengers of this, between whales and humans.

Personal State — The present state of human evolution, in which humans have developed a sense of individuality and a certain degree of self-determination, but have lost their unity with the Divine and are disconnected from spiritual realms.

Physical Body — The body made of flesh that we can all perceive, hear, touch, smell and taste.

Prepersonal State — A past stage of human evolution, in which humans had a much greater sense of unity with God and with nature, but a poor sense of their own individuality and little or no self-determination.

Sonar System — As with dolphins, it is the space between our eyebrows (called the third eye in several spiritual traditions). When awakened, it allows us to have vision and different ways to communicate and see.

Subtle Bodies — The astral, etheric and physical bodies and the higher self. A term for the perceived structure of our non-physical selves.

Third Eye — A fundamental gate that leads to the inner worlds. It allows us to know ourselves in a depth that surpasses all conventional methods based on analysis with the discursive mind.

Transpersonal State — The next stage of human evolution; a state in which the higher self is one with the Divine while retaining individuality (as opposed to prepersonal enlightenment in which all individuality has been dissolved).

Tune in — The dolphin way for people to perceive and communicate, using the *Sonar System* or *Third Eye*. It allows us to pick up other people's emotions, feelings and even thoughts.

Ultrasound — Human hearing or sonic range extends from 20–20 000 Hz, whilst that of dolphins extends from 100–150 000 Hz. Frequencies above 20 000 Hz are inaudible to us; the vibrations are known as ultrasound.

Water Baby — A baby born into water. They go from the water of the womb to the water of the bath. Many hospitals in Australia provide facilities to have water birth. It has been shown that water babies are far less fearful and argumentative. In short, they show the characteristics of human dolphins.

Will — The power by which consciousness achieves and manifests. An important quality for the shark or the dolphin.

INDEX

THE DOLPHIN SOCIETY

PO Box 2052 Clovelly 2031 Australia
Tel +61 2 9665 0712 Fax +61 2 9664 2018
Email william@hutch.com.au
Internet http://wwwhutch.com.au/~william/dolphins.htm

DECLARATION OF RIGHTS FOR WHALES AND DOLPHINS
Refer Page 52

In recognition of the special relationship that exists between cetaceans and humans we are seeking the extension of the Universal Declaration of Human Rights (United Nations 1948) to include whales and dolphins. We are presently collecting signatures in support of this declaration all over the world.

Please add YOUR name in support.

We the undersigned support the UNIVERSAL DECLARATION OF MARINE MAMMAL RIGHTS Charter One: Cetaceans (Whales and Dolphins)

FULL NAME	ADDRESS	SIGNATURE